LADY IN BOOMTOWN

VINTAGE WEST SERIES

Eureka and its Resources
by Lambert Molinelli, 1879

Report of Explorations Across the
Great Basin . . . in 1859
by Captain James H. Simpson, 1876

An Editor on the Comstock Lode
by Wells Drury, 1936

Frémont: Explorer for
a Restless Nation
by Ferol Egan, 1977

Sand in a Whirlwind:
The Paiute Indian War of 1860
by Ferol Egan, 1972

The Town That Died Laughing:
The Story of Austin, Nevada
by Oscar Lewis, 1955

Silver Kings . . . Lords of the
Nevada Comstock Lode
by Oscar Lewis, 1947

Wells, Fargo Detective:
A Biography of James B. Hume
by Richard Dillon, 1969

Sierra-Nevada Lakes
by George and Bliss Hinkle, 1949

Exploring the Great Basin
by Gloria Griffen Cline, 1963

High Sierra Country
by Oscar Lewis, 1955

I Remember Christine
by Oscar Lewis, 1942

Sagebrush Trilogy:
Idah Meacham Strobridge
and Her Works
*by Idah Meacham Strobridge,
1904, 1907, 1909*

The WPA Guide to 1930s Nevada
*by the Nevada Writers' Project
of the WPA, 1940*

A Kid on the Comstock:
Reminiscences
of a Virginia City Childhood
by John Taylor Waldorf, 1970

Lady in Boomtown: Miners and
Manners on the Nevada Frontier
by Mrs. Hugh Brown, 1968

LADY
IN
BOOMTOWN

MINERS AND MANNERS
ON THE NEVADA FRONTIER

by

Mrs. Hugh Brown

UNIVERSITY OF NEVADA PRESS
Reno and Las Vegas

VINTAGE WEST SERIES EDITOR: ROBERT E. BLESSE

This book was originally published by American West Publishing Company
in 1968, and a paperback edition was published by Ballantine Books in 1972.
This volume reproduces the American West edition except that the front
matter has been changed to reflect the new publisher.

The paper used in this book meets the requirements of American National
Standard for Information Sciences—Permanence of Paper for Printed Library
Materials, ANSI Z39.48-1984

Library of Congress Cataloging-in-Publication Data
Brown, Hugh, Mrs.
Lady in Boomtown : miners and manners on the Nevada frontier / by
Mrs. Hugh Brown ; introduction by Walter Van Tilburg Clark.
p.   cm. — (Vintage West series)
Reprint. Originally published: Palo Alto, Calif. : American West
Pub. Co., 1968.
ISBN 0-87417-169-5 (pbk. : alk. paper)
1. Tonopah (Nev.)—Social life and customs.   2. Goldfield (Nev.)—
Social life and customs.   3. Gold mines and mining—Nevada—
Tonopah—History—20th century.   4. Gold mines and mining—Nevada—
Goldfield—History—20th century.   5. Brown family.   I. Title.
II. Series.
F849.T6B7   1991
979.3'34—dc20   90-26195
                                                                      CIP

University of Nevada Press, Reno, Nevada 89557 USA
Copyright © 1968 Marjorie Anne Brown. All rights reserved
Cover design by Kaelin Chappell
Cover illustration by Susan Carolla Iannone
Printed in the United States of America

2   4   6   8   9   7   5   3   1

ACKNOWLEDGMENTS

A Lady in Boomtown was developed from notes I kept during the years I spent in Tonopah from 1904 to 1922. To awaken my memory of historical and political events, the librarian at the San Francisco Mechanics Library directed me to the file of current histories compiled by Mark Sullivan, a New York reporter.

Articles pertaining to Tonopah itself in current magazines and periodicals were fragmentary. When I discovered how difficult it was to find two statements that agreed about those very early days, I decided to trust my own memory, fortified by the many clippings I had saved from newspapers and by similar data from my husband's files.

I am immeasurably grateful to my friend David Myrick, a writer and compiler of western history, whose prolific notebooks helped me to be more accurate in some of my statements.

The statistics on Goldfield are from an article by Charles F. Spillman that appeared in the *Nevada News Letter* of January 1, 1916, a copy of which I had preserved. His figures corresponded to my own memory sufficiently for me to accept their accuracy.

During Tasker Oddie's lifetime we talked for many happy hours about the old days, and much I have written came out of those conversations. He also furnished me with campaign literature pertaining to himself and Key Pittman, together with magazine clippings about the battleship *Nevada*. All of these were returned to Senator Oddie, so I have no record of the published sources from which they were clipped.

Most of the gossip came to me through my brother and my brother-in-law, who joined us when Tonopah began to boom. Whenever either one of them picked up "off the street" an exciting bit of information, they shared it with me and I added it to my notes.

The photographs and snapshots I collected myself. For me the cluttered little gallery of E. W. Smith, the photographer who took most of the pictures, was a regular port-of-call. When the old man died, our friend Herman Albert was the public administrator, and he asked me if I would like to have Mr. Smith's pictures. I gladly went down to the littered room over the Oasis Saloon and thumbed through the vast number of prints. If I had thought of their future historical value, I would have preserved them all. Most of the photographs of people — leading citizens and holiday events — were acquired from Mr. Smith's studio.

TO

HUGH *and* MARSHALL *and* JERRIE

This is written for you. Primarily, of course, it is the story of your father and me during our youthful years in Nevada. But it is more than that, for to write of Tonopah and Goldfield from 1903 to 1922 is to describe the sunset rays of the old romantic West. We were the pioneers of the twentieth century — your father and mother and the colorful people we knew — carved in the round by memories of those wonderful years when it was such an engrossing experience to be a LADY IN BOOMTOWN.

San Francisco, California, 1968

INTRODUCTION

by Walter Van Tilburg Clark

The vast, mountainous, mostly arid, highly mineralized region that is now the state of Nevada has been the scene of two major mining excitements. Viewed distantly and generally, the two are alike in so many ways as to make a mere recital of their similarities a little embarrassing, like the telling of a tall story with no laughable point.

The first or northern excitement began with two discoveries made near the California border, was focused on two adjoining communities that grew up on the sites of those discoveries, lasted at boom-day pitch about twenty years, and gave rise during its first decade to widespread prospecting all across the north, to countless flash-in-the-pan rushes, and to the establishment of a dozen lesser but durable and productive camps. The second or southern excitement began twenty years after the first went into unquestionable decline, was focused in two neighboring towns near the western edge of the region, lasted about twenty years at boom-day pitch, and gave rise, during its first decade, to very much the same pattern of development, even to the number of importantly productive camps.

Each excitement produced hundreds of millions of dollars worth of gold and silver (to which the second, though remotely and not really within the framework of its rush, added nearly $170,000,000 in copper), and the focal camps of each were far and away the richest producers. Each excitement drew thousands of people into its region, did much to relieve a national depression, and gave material support to the nation in a major war. Each drew heavily upon San Francisco, eastern, and foreign capital, rewarded many of its out-of-state investors lavishly, and made first fortunes for a number of men who became thereafter widely known financiers and politicians. Each had many newspapers of its own and made national and international news repeatedly, not only with mining reports but with strikes, fires, plagues, murders, railroad celebrations, prize fights, swindles, stock booms, and stock crashes. During their heydays both had their full complement of local characters and distinguished visitors.

Enough. One could go on with the minor likenesses indefinitely. To cap their special similarities, the southern town of each focal pair was predominantly a gold producer and the northern a silver producer. The two gold towns failed ten years or more before their silver mates, and have now all but vanished in the most literal sense, the sense of people, streets, and buildings; and the two silver camps are livelier and more prosperous today than they have been at any time since the peak of their mining activities. When one adds that the second excitement is much closer to us, that it may well be the last such excitement the West or perhaps the world will ever see, that its surviving town is now several times as large as its northern counterpart, and that the great copper production that began during its era has continued undiminished and gives measured promise of going on for another hundred years or more, it would seem only reasonable to assume that its history, stories, growing legends, and remaining monuments ought to be at least as widely known as those of its predecessor.

Ought to be. But they aren't, not by a long shot.

The first excitement was the great Washoe or Comstock silver boom of 1860 to 1880; its focal towns were Virginia City and Gold Hill, and some of its better-known secondary camps were Bodie, Austin, Aurora, Unionville, Eureka, Hamilton, Treasure City, Pioche, Candeleria, and Silver Peak. As for the second excitement, *Lady in Boomtown* is a first-hand, various, often nostalgic, and sometimes carefully reticent account of its whole course, and it begins thus:

Hugh's voice at the other end of the telephone was serious and urgent. Would I meet him at the Occidental Hotel at four o'clock? It was near his office, and he was pressed for time.

"I'm going to Tonopah tonight, and I want to talk to you."

"Tonopah? Where's Tonopah?"

Just so. And if her husband-to-be (she was Miss Marjorie Moore then, and it will surprise no one who has lived in mining camps to learn that her family had roots in the wealth and tradition of the Comstock) had said "Goldfield" (he couldn't, it was not quite there yet) she would have had to echo him in the same bewildered way. Nor would anyone but a Nevadan or a truly devoted mining camp buff be likely to know anything about the secondary camps of the era such as Rhyolite (well, yes, many Death Valley tourists have seen its scanty remains — an old railroad station, a small house made of bottles, and a few fragments of foundations and walls), Bullfrog, Fairview, Wonder, Manhattan (there is still an old building there, or was a few years ago, which bears the intriguing sign "Manhattan Literary Society"), Round Mountain, Greenwater, Reveille, Johnny, Bellehelen, Bonnie Clare. Of all those secondary boomtowns only remote Ely, which is no ghost town at all, is known to many visitors, and that is because of its vast, still-working copper pit.

Why this almost unbelievable difference in repute between northern and southern mining regions, Virginia City and Tonopah? Place has something to do with it. Tonopah and the remnants of Goldfield (among which are a boarded-up stone school, a county courthouse, and a huge, empty, two-hundred-room hotel) are located on a main north-south highway between Las Vegas and Reno, but they stand about midway between those two cities, some two hundred miles from both. There is little else of tourist interest around them; the drive to them is long and, in summer, hot. Relatively few tourists use that route, and most of the regular business travelers between Reno and Las Vegas go by air. So Tonopah, though busy enough as the school, shopping, and amusement center of a very large ranching and mining district, the rest stop for a moderate number of travelers, and a link in the air-defense chain, is not drawing those who come to look.

Time may be even more important than place. The fact that the southern boom happened so much closer to the present actually militates against Tonopah and Goldfield in a number of ways. They are less known than they would be if they were older. Those who relish the mild quaintness of early twentieth-century building will find much to please them in Tonopah, but those so drawn are relatively few, and a great many communities all over the United States still have buildings of that vintage. Tonopah simply does not look as picturesque as Virginia City, with its arcaded boardwalks, spool-railed balconies, gingerbread trim, pressed-tin ceilings eighteen or twenty feet high, ornate backbars, crystal chandeliers, and suspended cranberry lamps, which make it easy to imagine ghosts in frock coats and bustles and to revive the sense of what one likes to believe was a less troubled, more spacious, and more optimistic age than our own.

Virginia City has had an advantage, too, in that it was not only a major silver camp, but the first silver camp in North America. Its mines were not only quoted on the San Francisco exchange, they were the reason that exchange was founded. It was the Comstock excitement which quickly changed western Utah Territory into Nevada Territory and then, as quickly again, into the State of Nevada. Comstock men whose names echo for us played dominant roles in the formulation of the state constitution. During the early, wasteful years of constant mining litigation (all the original claims were recorded, if at all, according to the surface rules of California placer mining, and proved meaningless when deeper mining began to follow the angle of the lode and the trend of discovered veins and ledges), Comstock attorneys and geologists worked out deep mining definitions and laws which have been in force in the state ever since and which set national precedents. Comstock mining ran into unique difficulties with heat, underground water, ventilation, timbering, reduction, and recovery, which led to the development of so many inventions and new methods that Virginia City became a mining school to the world. The Comstock was witness to the first passing of the Pony Express riders, became a main stop on the first regular overland stage routes, helped to string the first transcontinental telegraph line, and built the first short line railroad in the state, the Virginia and Truckee, to meet the first transcontinental railroad, the Central Pacific. There could be no historical firsts of that sort for Tonopah and Goldfield, and their mining laws and practices could be no more than continuations of those established on the Comstock.

The awareness of these differences has been almost as important as the differences themselves. The early comers to the Comstock knew they were making history, and that sense of history led, from the beginning, to a desire to record and keep mementoes. Most of the Comstock bars are little museums, with glassware, firearms, paintings, ore exhibits, mining tools, bar books (Red Tom — $12.50; Black Tom — $17.00; Three Finger Tom — $22.75), hotel registers, and innumerable photographs of the city in different stages, of Fourth of July parades, of notable hoisting works and mills, of V&T trains, of prominent personalities, of mustached miners, bare chested and with folded arms, seated in tiers like football teams. Tonopah and Goldfield knew they were making mining history, but they also knew that they were not, in anything like the same degree, making any other kind, and in comparison with the Comstock they have done little to preserve their records or relics.

Distance has lent enchantment to the Comstock as it has not to Tonopah. Those "good old days" on the Comstock, like the still more celebrated days of the gold rush, were neither as spacious nor as optimistic as the popular accounts of them suggest. Popular accounts have a way of culling out the unpleasant, glamorizing the spectacular, concentrating on the good fortune of a small minority, ignoring the misfortunes of the majority, and stopping when the decline sets in. Actually, Virginia City and San Francisco (the supply towns were the real boomtowns of the gold rush), and the gold camps even more, have an appalling record of unpunished killings, vindictive fire-settings, vigilante actions, racial hostilities, fatal accidents, hopeless poverty on the doorstep of outsize wealth, swindles, embezzlements, deaths by tuberculosis, cholera, and smallpox — anything in the file of crime and disaster.

Hatred, violence, prejudice, despair, death when they bear upon people wearing clothes unlike ours become picturesque and oddly fascinating. The war in which the Comstock played such an important part, for instance, was the Civil War, and the part it played was not simply the sending of much bullion from afar to the Union treasury. That war was fought — politically, legally, and often in actual shooting affrays — right on the Comstock, all during the time it was being fought on battlefields in the South, and for nearly a generation beyond that time. Those conflicts are very colorful stuff, looked back on. How can Tonopah or Goldfield compete? The war to which they supplied financial aid, World War I, has already been more forgotten than the Civil War, and it left no local scars or legends. How are Tonopah and Goldfield, in modern or nearly-modern dress, with much more careful and orderly mining, and with the autobus soon replacing the stagecoach, and the beat-up touring car the prospector's burro, to match such yarns as the great Comstock fire of 1875, such personalities as Eilly Orum and Sandy Bowers?

The fact is that, given half a chance, they can; known, they reveal their own picturesque color. They had a ruthless contest between monopolistic mine owners and a miners' union egged on by IWW agitators, which led to the use of federal troops. And the most immediate cause of that trouble was the attempt of the owners to stop "highgrading," the stealing by miners of spectacular high-grade or "jewelry" ore, ore so rich that it could be easily and very profitably reduced and "fenced" through unscrupulous assayers. (The Comstock never saw such ore as that.) And fifty-two blocks of Goldfield did burn one night, but after the boom was over, and so they were never rebuilt as Virginia City was after the fire of 1875. And there was Tex Rickard's shoot-'em-up hoax for a visiting authoress. All of this, and much else, is the stuff of legend, but it hasn't even become well-known story yet. The high-button coat and bowler hat or visored cap of the businessman and the leather puttees and flat-brimmed campaign hat of the mining engineer of the twentieth century boom don't catch the eye as the frock coat and brass-buttoned red shirt do. But certainly those narrow, high-wheeled, brass-lamp cars have become good vintage already. And kids, at least, are already laughing at bowler hats and leather puttees. The Tonopah vista has lengthened almost to the picturesque, and the romantic is not far beyond that.

Though the Comstock had more of everything than the southern boom, more gold and silver, more people, more famous mines and notable figures and events, no one should disparage what happened in Tonopah. A conservative professional estimate credits the major camps of the southern boom with a total of about $365,000,000, including $167,000,000 in copper from Ely. The same source gives Tonopah $109,000,000 and Goldfield $80,250,000 — quite enough to create a major frenzy of excitement.

Nobody can give accurate population figures for boom camps. They have too many floating characters, and they can boom and die between one census and the next. But one reasonable estimate credits the southern excitement with having brought thirty thousand new people into the state, and gives Goldfield, at its peak the largest town of that boom, a maximum of something like fifteen thousand. A handful of the southern figures acquired more than local reputations; a few more have survived in the state annals; and two, Senator Key Pittman and Senator Patrick McCarran, have become nationally known. Here again there is reason to honor the people who made the southern boom, for in good part their obscurity is a result of the fact that they were not given to the flamboyant gestures and mouthings of the Comstock big shots, and that they *were* given to putting their wealth and political influence to work for Nevada. By contrast, the Comstock wealth was all drained off to San Francisco and big eastern cities, and even to Europe, where it kept on making the news, both financially and socially; and the Comstock political big-wigs, when they weren't in Washington, made their actual headquarters at the Palace Hotel in San Francisco, and showed up in Nevada for only a week or so before each election.

We know the Comstock legends better than those of Tonopah because the doings of the Comstock were abundantly and colorfully recorded in their own time. Such papers as the *Territorial Enterprise,* the *Union,* and the *Chronicle* of Virginia City, the Gold Hill *Evening*

News, the Carson *Appeal,* the *Reese River Reveille* of Austin, and the Bodie *Index-Miner* were widely read in their own time and are now abundantly searched; and the names of the men who made them so lively with personal feuds, political furies, tall stories, whimsies, unbridled patriotism, fulsome and satirical treatments of theatrical and social events — Goodman, Goodwin, McCarthy, Dan De Quille, Mark Twain, Alf Doten, Will Booth, Sam Davis, Lying Jim Townsend — were then and still are names to conjure with. Many of those Comstock newspapermen, and many visitors as well, wrote novels, factual accounts, humorous stories, about the Comstock, the region, and their personal experiences in both. Most western readers, certainly, know Dan De Quille's *The Big Bonanza,* and most Americans of whatever bent know Mark Twain's *Roughing It.* In addition, histories and mining studies appeared, and a steady and ever-increasing flow of writing of all sorts has drawn upon these originals ever since, not only for substance but for manner and tone as well. There can be little question, in fact, that the present notion of the Comstock's optimism has come into being more because of the way the Comstock spoke of itself than because of what it actually did.

And in this matter, the day-by-day account and the growth of the legend, Tonopah and Goldfield have fared worst of all. Not even Bill Booth's Tonopah *Times-Bonanza,* the most readable of their newspapers, compares for color with either his father's *Reese River Reveille* or Jim Townsend's *Index-Miner,* let alone with the *Territorial Enterprise.* The flair and impulse of the earlier pistol-and-horsewhip journalism never developed in the southern boom, and opinion on serious matters, both by custom and out of necessity, was much more carefully put. So the southern papers have not picked up a following of enthusiasts. What is more, so far as this writer knows, only one book-length, factual study of the southern boom has appeared so far (mining and geological studies in bulletin form are plentiful, but they are of little interest to the general reader). The one general study is Russell Elliott's *Nevada's 20th Century Mining Boom* (University of Nevada Press, 1966). The book you hold in your hand is the only other account of any sort.

Never mind. That is precisely its value. The stuff of legend is in that southern boom, however unknown and undeveloped. Its papers, though relatively small and dull, are loaded with the substance of that legend. Mrs. Brown is opening the way to its becoming known. In her pages you will read of the famous leases of the first excitement, the Hays-

Monette, Sandstrom, Jumbo, January, White Horse, Red Top, Mohawk, and meet the notable personalities of that time, many of whom turn out to be nearly legendary already, at least to Nevadans, and some of whom will be known to most Americans: Tasker Oddie, Key Pittman, Jim Butler, Zeb Kendall, George Wingfield, George Nixon, Noble Getchell, Emmett Boyle, John Sparks, Bill Booth, Arthur Buel, Clara Kimball Young, Tex Rickard, Wyatt Earp, Jack Dempsey, Elinor Glyn — it is a considerable and various list.

And there are plenty of events as well, recorded here and still to be recorded, and some of them are of a kind that can no longer take place: a stagecoach journey, a party in the depths of a mine, a miners' drilling contest, a short-line railroad celebration, an old-fashioned, all-out Fourth of July. Throughout Mrs. Brown's story there runs a strong personal sense first of the exultation of boom and then of the poignant despair of bust. It is a true boom-day account, in fact and in spirit, and a fine beginning for the so-far overlooked Tonopah-Goldfield legend.

Walter Van Tilburg Clark
Reno, Nevada; June 1968

"They tell me you're an old-timer around here." The man smiled as he looked me over. "You certainly don't look like a pioneer."

"Oh, but I am." I answered proudly. "I came here on a stagecoach in February, 1904."

"Somebody told me I ought to look you up. I wish I had been here in the beginning," he added with a note of regret. "This place is all that is left of the old West, isn't it?"

HUGH'S VOICE AT THE OTHER END of the telephone was serious and urgent. Would I meet him at the Occidental Hotel at four o'clock? It was near his office, and he was pressed for time.

"I'm going to Tonopah tonight, and I want to talk to you."

"*Tonopah?* Where's Tonopah?"

For sixty years people have been asking the same question. Only those who have been there seem to be aware of its existence.

"It's a mining camp in southern Nevada," Hugh answered. "They've discovered ore there — gold and silver. A boom's on."

Like any other young lady in San Francisco in 1903 who wanted to meet a man in a downtown hotel, I had to request my mother's permission, which she gave with just the right amount of reluctance. I suspected that she was not unmindful of the fact that Hugh Brown was a very eligible young man, a graduate of Stanford University law school, serving the usual internship in a prominent firm, Campbell, Metson, and Campbell. If I was in love with him, it might quiet the agitation caused by my famous uncle, Theodore Roberts, a leading character actor of the era who was determined to lure me to New York for a career on the stage. No lady became an actress, my family insisted, even if she had talent. But, after all, I had already been graduated from Mills Seminary, and I was eighteen and not always sweetly amenable.

Hugh met me at the door of the hotel looking excited and happy — a tall, slender young man in a light grey suit with a blue stock tie. We walked up a flight of red-carpeted stairs to the "Ladies' Parlor," a large elegant room hung with dark red drapery and filled with massive furniture upholstered in the red plush and fringe made fashionable two decades before by riches that poured into San Francisco from Virginia City.

Briefly Hugh told me what had happened. A prospector had discovered rich ore out in the middle of the Nevada desert, and the rush was on. Hugh's firm had decided to open a law office there, and to his delight, he had been selected to represent the firm in the new town — Tonopah. He'd be gone maybe a year, not a day longer. With no further preliminaries he plunged on: would I marry him? I raised my eyes to his sweet serious face.

Of course I would.

He waved his hand to include the drawing room. "It won't be like this," he said. "It will mean hard work and rough living, but it will be exciting. There'll be no running water, and there'll be Indians."

With the wide smile that brought out the characteristic lines around his mouth, he added, "And you'd better get used to canned milk, for that's all you'll get." I threw back my head and laughed with the confidence of extreme youth.

Then we became grave as he held out his hand. "My bags are downstairs, and my ferry leaves in thirty minutes."

With a glance around the room — there were only two other people in the parlor — Hugh drew a newspaper from his pocket, unfolded it, and whispered, "Here, take this end. I haven't kissed my promised bride."

I took the edge of the newspaper, and we held it up as a shield. For the first time I kissed my future husband. Then he touched the chatelaine watch pinned on my breast and turned it over to read the inscription: *Animo et fide* (WITH COURAGE AND FAITH). It was my mother's motto, engraved on the watch she had given me as a graduation gift. As I look back to that moment, with more than sixty years between that time and this, I know Hugh needed the motto more than I, for this young man of twenty-eight was about to assume the hazard of taking to the frontier a bride of nineteen, a girl who had always been completely sheltered and was entirely unprepared for hardship — trained for nothing except how to be a lady.

Ten months later Hugh returned to San Francisco. We were married in my sister's home in a radiant little ceremony with music and flowers, white satin and lace. The following evening we boarded the Southern Pacific train for Reno. The first night of our traveling honeymoon was spent in the Golden Hotel in Reno, comfortable except for the fact that it was right next to the railroad racks. The Southern Pacific engines snorted and whistled and rang bells and switched freight cars that crashed together all night long.

The next morning we went on to Carson City by the Virginia and Truckee, whose shining brass-trimmed engines are famous in western railroad history. A few passengers, ourselves included, changed trains at Carson and rode as far as Mound House, where we lost a few more travelers and boarded the Carson & Colorado, a hesitant, jolting narrow-gauge that was to carry us south to a place called Hawthorne. All day the toy train lurched through miles and miles of sand and sagebrush, constantly spraying us with cinders and dust. The only other moving things on the landscape were the bands of wild horses whirling away into the distance as our train approached.

At long intervals we stopped at way-stations, nothing more than a group of whitewashed cabins protected from winter wind and summer sun by three or four towering cottonwoods. It was February and we had left the spring well advanced in California; but in Nevada it was still winter, and the columns of these majestic trees, golden in the winter sun, were a brilliant contrast to the flat, tan country through which we traveled.

About two o'clock in the afternoon the train wheezed to a stop at Waubuska, where we were to have lunch. In desert travel, Hugh said, Waubuska food was famous. We had had nothing to eat since six o'clock that morning, and anything would have been acceptable; but here was the welcome refreshment of steak and canned corn, apple pie, coffee, and excellent homemade bread. What a treat!

After lunch I had my first opportunity to examine the Indians who were grouped around every little desert station. The men were lean and brown, dressed in overalls and faded blue shirts, with black hair overlong, straggling from under broad black felt hats of ancient origin. Their fat, bunchy squaws were still wrapped in blankets like their grandmothers, with brilliant handkerchiefs tied around their weather-lined faces, the inevitable baby in a papoose basket slung on their backs or propped up against the station-house wall. The stolid, silent little creatures seemed utterly oblivious to the flies crawling unmolested around their eyes and mouths. It all seemed so close to the savage — as indeed it was, for only a generation earlier the Paiutes had been on the warpath. Now they were idle and weak, sunning themselves in the lee of a whitewashed wall. Coming toward us along the station platform was a man whom I had noticed at the dining table, extremely handsome and with regular features, like a Remington painting. As he drew nearer, Hugh introduced him as Key Pittman and promised that I would be hearing a lot about him in the future. Mr. Pittman pulled off his wide black Stetson, extended his hand in a strong, warm handclasp, and paid me a hearty compliment. As he looked down at me from dark brown eyes, I felt the pull of his unmistakable charm.

Just then the conductor called "A-all *aboard!*" and we all obeyed.

As the train got under way, a large man, about fifty and older than most of these travelers, came through the car. I suspected that he was looking for us, as he had been smiling at me all during lunch. Hugh introduced him as Judge Kenneth Jackson from Texas, who was on his way to Tonopah to take part in some "apex litigation." I reflected quickly that, as the wife of a mining camp lawyer, I might as well begin to make myself familiar with the local language.

In answer to my query, I learned that apex litigation had to do with establishing legal ownership underground at mining sites. In hard rock mining, such as that in the Tonopah district, veins of ore appear on the surface, usually as wide strips of metal-impregnated rock. Veins extend down into the earth on a slant because of ground upheavals during prehistoric eras. According to mining law, the company that owns the claim where the vein appears on the surface can follow the vein and mine it out as long as it doesn't "fault," that is break off or change direction. Veins sometimes wander underground, peter out in thin threads, or disappear entirely. It can be very expensive to hire engineers and lawyers to establish legal ownership underground or to prove that neighboring companies are not poaching on one another.

Judge Jackson, seemed very gratified by my interest. As it turned out, he was to stay in the camp for several years and figured somewhat in my life.

Among the passengers on the little train was Captain Case, a man older than most of the others, bronzed, lined, and weatherworn. The captain was a man of distinguished background. He not only had a degree in engineering from the University of Heidelberg, but he carried a dramatic scar down the left side of his face, acquired in the gentle art of dueling during his student days. Now he was superintendent of one of the mines in Tonopah.

Captain Case had once been an Indian fighter along the Mexican border. In 1903 Indian skirmishes were only a few years behind us; and when I was about sixteen, I had devoured the picturesque frontier novels of Captain Charles King, whose characters and locations dealt with army life along the border. Captain Case was a man who could tell just such yarns from his own experience, and on that journey I listened with fascination. Today, when I see a Western created around Indians, good and bad, and United States soldiers, also in the same categories, a wave of nostalgia sweeps over me, and I am a bride again listening to the romantic captain as the fussy little train takes us deeper into the Nevada desert.

With Captain Case was John Kirchen, one of the most brilliant mining engineers ever to come to Nevada. He could reach out with his diamond drill and pick up a lost vein as if he could see it. I discovered he was also an excellent conversationalist, and his explanation of the development of the mines aroused an interest in me that I never lost.*

About seven o'clock, terribly tired, we arrived at the station called Hawthorne, where passengers and crew were to spend the night. This being my wedding journey, I wore a blue "going away" suit and a hat of solid red poppies. Hugh said my hat shed a glow in the darkness "second only to my eyes." But even the pretty compliment wasn't enough to raise my flagging enthusiasm, nor did the sight of the hotel — a square black blob in the darkness with a thin sickly light from somewhere in the interior — do anything to reassure me.

Indeed, my unfavorable impression was justified. Our "dinner" was set out on a large oblong table covered with dark brown oilcloth. It was lighted from above by a metal kerosene lamp with a wide, bell-like paper shade, which threw a dim glow down over the table. Just under the lamp a big round shadow spread over the food and shifted eerily as the winter wind swept in when the door was opened. Beyond the rim of the lamplight, the room stretched away into the depths of night shadow. Passengers and crew scuffed into the room, scraped kitchen chairs over the bare floor, and sat down at the one big table. Everything we ate was greasy and tasteless.

Hugh ate the boiled beef, dried-up tomatoes, and stiff, crumbly biscuits with apparent relish. As I had known him, he had been rather fastidious, but ten months of mining camp life had taught him to eat what was set in front of him — or else. I was hungry and glad to have food of any kind. I drifted alone into a little box of a room with big-patterned maroon wallpaper and a few sagging upholstered chairs, which served as a parlor. There I found a piano. I sat down and played the sweet, sentimental songs I was accustomed to sing for my friends at home in San Francisco —"The Four Leaf Clover," "Forgotten," "Little Boy Blue," "Glow Worm." The hotelkeeper's wife came into the room, a large, handsome brunette with a pompadour and fringe bang.

After standing there listening for a moment, she said, "You're Mrs. Hugh Brown, aren't you?" The falling inflection demanded no reply.

I nodded and smiled.

"You haven't been married very long." Again the falling inflection

*Today, just off Highway 95 as one approaches Tonopah, there is a square monument of native stone, about five feet high. Under this cairn lie John Kirchen's ashes. By his request, his final resting place is the desert he loved and from which his genius extracted so many millions.

of a statement of fact.

"No, I haven't," I answered promptly. Only two days, but I kept that information to myself.

"Are you going to Tonopah?" This time the question was direct.

"Yes," I replied lightly as I played on.

She looked at me steadily for a moment, and then an expression of sadness came into her eyes. Young as I was, I realized this desert woman was looking into the life ahead of me with eyes of experience, and the brooding pity in her face struck across my happiness like a chill wind. In my heart I resented her judgment. I was young, true. And inexperienced. But I was enthusiastic and in love. Why shouldn't I be happy?

Then Hugh appeared and we retired to our room. Our journey would be resumed at four o'clock in the morning. I looked at the bedding and shuddered; but I knew we had to have rest, so I did get into bed. However, in a few minutes I was conscious of something crawling. This I couldn't endure! So, sitting upright in an old Morris chair, wrapped in my heavy coat and with Hugh's overcoat on my knees, I managed to slip off to sleep.

It was still night when we were roused by a heavy knocking on the door. We dressed quickly, for the room was dead cold and there was no hot water. In the same dark room where we had dined, the Chinese cook offered us something that passed for coffee and two eggs cooked, mercifully, in their shells. But at least the room was warm, and we did get the chill out of us before we stepped out onto the station platform. There, drawn up and ready for departure, was the train that would carry us to the next way station — Sodaville — where we would transfer to the stagecoach that would take us the last sixty-five miles to Tonopah.

In the east a faint green glow told us sunrise was not too far off. All around me in the darkness were eerie shadows of men, bundles of tents and blankets, and piles of freight. By this time I realized I was the only woman in the party, and my spirits rose with the novelty of the occasion. The air was filled with the smell of burning cottonwood. The odor was like incense, and I was enchanted. Through all my desert years and even today, when I smell burning cottonwood, I am back in that early morning when I stepped out of the shack hotel at Hawthorne.

Day was breaking when we arrived at Sodaville, three rough-board cabins and a stable clustered haphazardly around a well, a way station in the middle of nowhere. As the train creaked and wheezed to a stop, with one last jolt by which to remember the journey, the conductor yelled:

"Sodaville! Change for all points in the world."

He was certainly right. There was no place to go but out. As I stepped into the sharp morning air, I scanned the horizon. I saw nothing but miles of sand and sage, with a slender ribbon of road disappearing amid the sand dunes, only to reappear on top of the next rise, and then be gone again. The low hills in the middle distance built up to pink, snow-capped mountains miles away. And in the foreground, its outlines softened by the half-light of sunrise, was the stagecoach with its six horses already in harness.

Here, I thought with excitement, was the same kind of conveyance that had been held up by desperadoes on just such roads all through western history. The driver, wrapped in a short canvas coat lined with sheepskin, stood by his lead horse with the long whip in his hand. He was a picturesque ruffian from a distance, but when we got close enough to see his eyes from under the long, shaggy eyebrows, I realized that he was greeting us with a smile from the mildest face in the world.

The baggage was stowed on the rack at the rear and also piled high on top of the stage. The process took some time, so Hugh had an opportunity to introduce me to some of our other traveling companions, among whom was Zeb Kendall — "the 'biggest' promoter in camp," Hugh said — a string bean of a man well over six feet tall, with a stoop men often acquire who are reticent by nature and too tall to be inconspicuous. Next was Mr. Harry Ramsey. Hugh introduced him without comment, but whispered to me later that he was one of the famous gunmen of the West with several recent notches on his shootin' iron. I took another look at him and saw only a quiet, completely colorless and inconspicuous man. I felt quite let down.

With the customary chivalry of the desert, these men treated me with overwhelming courtesy. For example, I was invited to sit outside, high up on the box seat with the driver, along with Zeb Kendall and Mr. Ramsey. I was tempted to accept, for I would have loved to ride up there even for a few miles. However, the day was very cold, and Hugh thought I would be more comfortable inside. So I was wedged between Captain Case and Mr. Kirchen, with Hugh facing me between Key Pittman and Judge Jackson. Midst much jangling and jerking of harness, we began the sixty-five mile journey into Tonopah, where, barring broken axle or a mud hole, we would arrive by midnight.

We started off in high spirits, full of conversation. The gentlemen were curious about my pioneer grandfather, old Captain Roberts, who had come around the Horn in command of his own ship, arriving in San Francisco Bay under full sail in April '49. In answer to their queries, I told of my grandmother's trip across the Isthmus of Panama, on foot and carrying a fifteen-month-old baby in her arms.

"And where had she come from?" someone asked.

"From Mobile. My grandfather was master of a sailing ship that plied between Mobile and New York; and on a trip they made to New York, my grandmother and her mother sailed with handsome young Captain Roberts. Off Key West they ran into one of those terrible storms that rage around that area. My grandfather ordered all passengers below deck, but my grandmother wanted to stay up and watch the excitement. So — the story goes — Grandfather lashed her to one of the masts and let her stay for a few hours. That was the beginning of their romance. He thought any girl who had that much pluck was worth going after."

Judge Jackson turned his kindly eyes on me. "That's a good heritage," he said gravely. "It ought to help."

Of course, much of the talk was of politics, a subject about which I knew nothing, although I recognized some of the names flashing through the conversation. For instance, I knew about John Hay, because he had been President Lincoln's private secretary and had written so eloquently about his great friend. However, I was a bit hazy about the "open door" in China, for which Mr. Hay, as Theodore Roosevelt's Secretary of State, seemed to be presently responsible.

Also, as we covered the miles that day, I heard the name of a young East Indian zealot who was carrying on single-handed warfare with the British Empire. That name, which forty years later was world famous, was Gandhi.

As the lengthening shadows made the sagebrush seem to take on added height, the swaying stagecoach became almost unbearable. There are two leather straps around the back axle of a stage that keep the springs from rising past a certain height. Every chuck hole — and there were many — would send us into the air; then the straps would stop us with a terrible jolt. After a few hours each rise and fall became torture. When the lumbering vehicle swung around one of the many curves, not even the tightness with which we were wedged against one another could keep us from swaying.

At dusk we drew into another oasis where food was served; the horses were changed, and we were allowed a half hour's welcome relaxation. In the glow of the sunset, crowded into the stage again but refreshed, we began to sing. We started with all the old standbys: "Sweet Marie," "Annie Roonie," and "Old Kentucky Home." Dick José was the popular ballad singer of that year, singing "Silver Threads among the Gold," "Dear Old Girl," and "Nellie Was a Lady" in his sweet high tenor; so of course these songs came to mind, as well as hit tunes from the light operas of 1901. The patriotic songs we sang were from the Civil War, for strangely, the Spanish-American War, from which we had so lately emerged, had not produced any songs of its own.

Slowly the night settled down; slowly the hours wore on. We became more serious and quieter; to the accompaniment of scuffling hoofs and harness rattle, beloved old hymns floated softly over the still air: "Rock of Ages," "Lead Kindly Light," "Onward Christian Soldiers."

At last the twinkling lights of Tonopah began to flicker in the distance. About midnight we jangled into town, up the main street, and with a quick right turn, came to a stop in front of the post office. Much to my surprise, there was quite a crowd of men to greet us. Even at this late hour the arrival of the stage was an event.

THE SHOUTING AND COMMOTION hardly penetrated the haze of fatigue and dizziness that surrounded me. I was so stiff from the jolting ride that Hugh had to hold me up for a few moments after I had climbed down from the coach. Fortunately, I soon recovered, for we had a rather difficult walk ahead to reach the house that Hugh had rented for us.

We said goodbye to our traveling companions, Hugh shouldered our bags, and we trudged away up the hill. After the long confinement, it was a relief to stretch our legs and within twenty minutes we were mounting the rough steps of the little cottage, which looked like an owl in the moonlight, with two windows for eyes and a narrow door for a beak.

The door was not locked. Hugh dropped our bags and reached for the light cord, then gathered me into his arms as we stepped into our new home. I forgot I was tired and forgot the twinge of fear I had felt in Hawthorne. The light bulb in the center of the room danced on the end of its cord as if in exuberant greeting.

Suddenly I was conscious of a sound on the night air, a faint, soft sigh. *"Chew, chee-chew,"* with a slight accent on the first long syllable and a quickening on the next two. To my curious question, Hugh explained that it was the donkey engine down at the Desert Queen. I was amazed that work continued at the mines all night. "Are they in such a hurry to get the gold out?"

"Three shifts in twenty-four hours," Hugh told me. "If you had millions under the ground, wouldn't you be in a hurry to get them out?" Then he explained that this was not a gold camp. This was silver mining. Of course, there was some gold in the ore, and it helped to raise the values.

I looked out over the little town where clusters of lights around a mine shaft told of unceasing activity, although the night was more than half gone. It seemed as if I, too, could not wait for morning to begin the new life, for which I was so little equipped by anything but a rugged inheritance.

Morning on the desert dawned clear and frightfully cold. I was glad to obey Hugh's suggestion that I stay in bed while he started a fire in the sheet-iron stove, which was soon giving off a roar out of all proportion to its diminutive size. I hopped out of bed, grabbed my clothes, and rushed into the living room to dress before its warmth.

What I could see of the house by daylight reassured me. It was cozy and clean. I learned that it was typical of all the others in the camp: three rooms inside a board-and-batten box, with a screened porch on the rear. There was a good matting rug on the floor of the main room, with a cabinet of sorts where one could store everything from dishes to firewood, a tiny sheet-iron stove, a table with four rush chairs, and an old-fashioned leather sofa, not to overlook the colored calendar on the wall. In the bedroom were an iron bed, a washstand, and an old-fashioned dark brown bureau. The kitchen was negligible except for a huge barrel of water in one corner and a wood-burning range.

But, thank goodness, we had electric light and a telephone. As soon as the camp had become an established fact, power lines were strung two hundred miles across the mountains from Inyo, California, to furnish electric power for the mines, so from its inception the town had light and telephones.

Meanwhile, Hugh built a fire in the kitchen range where *I* was expected presently to produce breakfast! By the time I was dressed Hugh had water boiling — water dipped from the barrel in the corner. I looked at that range with awe.

"You'll have to get breakfast," I said. "I've never made coffee in my life."

Hugh made the coffee. At least he took some coffee and did something to it. If there had been an atom of guile in his make-up, I would have suspected him of playing a trick on me, for the coffee he made that morning was unbelievably bad. The thought came to me that if this was the stuff he had been making for himself all these months, it was certainly up to me to learn to cook. I couldnt stand *this* coffee!

After breakfast I slipped into my heavy coat, and for a moment we stood silent at the door, breathing deeply of the sparkling desert air. Our house was well up on the side of a mountain, and directly opposite was another mountain. Between them, in the canyon and climbing both sides, lay the little rough-board town. Snuggled in among the shacks and dwarfing them were mine shafts with hoists and ore dumps. West of town the desert stretched for miles to the horizon, which was edged with the snowcapped Sierra Nevada. In the opposite direction, to the east, a curving scratch indicated a road winding up the draw and disappearing over the edge of the hill.

I asked Hugh why the town had been built on the sides of this steep canyon. Hugh shook his head. The canyon was not so steep. When I got down into the town, I would see that ages of cloud bursts running down the canyon had levelled off a perfect townsite. The outcroppings where the original discovery had been made were midway up the side of the mountain opposite. All the location claims had been laid out there, but tents "set" better on the level, so the first settlers naturally had put up their tents on the floor of the canyon. As cabins replaced tents, footpaths followed the land level and became streets. They would probably remain the way they were as long as the camp lasted.

Do the two mountains have names? I wondered.

"Darn right they have. That's Mount Oddie opposite, where all the mine shafts are," Hugh continued. "And those red buildings over there about even with our eyes mark the Tonopah Mining Company. The strike was made just below there where you see that dump of grey waste. Remember my telling you about Tasker Oddie? That's his mine."

I did indeed remember. I had not met Tasker Oddie yet, but I felt I knew him, for Hugh's letters in the past ten months had been full of him. Hugh next pointed out the buildings of the Montana Tonopah and the North Star mines. We were living on Mount Brougher, named for Wilse Brougher. I would hear about him later. Hugh took his watch from his pocket. "I must go. I run a law shop, you know, not an information bureau."

I laughed as I kissed him goodbye, and then drew my coat tighter around me and stood for a while looking at the landscape — line upon line of running color, tan, henna, lavender, brown. But no green. Not a tree. Not a shrub. A faint odor floated by me reminiscent of Christmas, a spicy something I afterward recognized as sage.

I had been born in San Francisco, had lived all my life in the green fragrance of that moisture-laden air, and yet this dry, rarified atmosphere, so sparkling, this vast expanse of open country were overpoweringly lovely. Looking down on the quaint rough-board town below, I heard the soft, insistent chatter of the donkey engine. That woman in Hawthorne who pitied me was a fool.

The days that followed were a kaleidoscope of vivid impressions. The daylight captivated me and the night enchanted me. Under the desert moonlight the hills looked as if they had been cut out of cardboard, as if a light had been planted down behind them somewhere to intensify their contour against the night sky.

Added to the fascination of the pastel landscape was the friendly charm of the people, the first impression of which I had experienced on the stage trip into Tonopah. As each day passed, I was warmed by the friendship with which they met Hugh's bride. My first caller, soon after my arrival, was Mrs. Albert Stock, who lived just below me on the hill. She was the wife of an engineer at one of the mines. Mrs. Stock asked me to forgive her for coming so quickly, but she wanted me to know I had neighbors and didn't want me to be lonely.

Later, when I learned Jen Stock's story, I knew why she was concerned for loneliness. When she married Mr. Stock, he was superintendent of a salt works near Sodaville, and the Stocks lived there for many years. All the workers on the salt marsh were Indians, and Jen was the only white woman for fifty miles around. She knew what loneliness could do to a woman.

But that very night I learned there was another kind of neighborliness not quite so pleasant. After dinner I was in my kitchen wiping the dishes, while Hugh was sitting in the living room with a book. A terrific din erupted all around the house, a combination of tin cans, bells, horns — anything that could make a noise. Dreadfully shocked and frightened, I rushed to my husband for protection, but Hugh sat calmly smoking his pipe with a smile of amusement on his face. I was trembling with fear.

He took his pipe from his mouth and told me quietly not to be alarmed. It was just a shivaree.

I had heard the word before, but never expected to be subjected to such disrespectful treatment. My eyes filled with tears of humiliation and then anger.

Voices began calling, "We want to see the bride! Come on out or we'll come in!"

"Don't take it so seriously," Hugh said, laughing at me. "You'll have to show up, so you'd better dry your eyes and smile. It's just a frontier joke." At last he opened the door and waved for our tormentors to come in.

The din stopped, and about twenty young men poured into the house. I swallowed my fury and smiled and bowed. At Hugh's suggestion I brought from the kitchen what few cookies I had, and Hugh turned his pockets inside out and threw his wallet on the table. The men scooped up about twenty dollars and all the cookies; then yelling, "Much obliged! Happy days!" they went off noisily down the hill, leaving me spent with excitement.

Another early visitor who gave my new life some brushed-in color was Mrs. Hank Knight, a thin, homely woman with a chirpie sweetness that made her very attractive. From Mrs. Knight I gained my first realization of the comradeship of the frontier. At the turn of the century towns were far apart. Travel was by stage or buckboard, slow and hard, as I had experienced. I wondered how people could know one another so well. Mrs. Knight, who was considerably older than I, knew people all over the state, and she knew them by their first names. Many native Nevadans had come to Tonopah, of course, but I remember being delighted and somehat startled by our conversation on the day she called. When I mentioned someone I had just met, she would look at me questioningly for a moment. Then her eyes would kindle and she would drawl, "Oh. Oh, yes. You mean *Sarah* So-and-So. Why, yes, of course. I knew her when she was little. She used to get lost in the sagebrush, and her mother tied a sheep bell around her neck so they could find her."

Both Mrs. Knight and her husband had much of the Old West still clinging to them, which even in my youth was fast disappearing. There was, too, a code of frontier ethics Mr. Knight displayed for me. He was a really fine person, a handsome old chap with beautiful grey hair and a short white chin-beard, which made him look like a Mormon bishop. But Mr. Knight ran a saloon. I had met him one night at the Mizpah Club shortly after our arrival in Tonopah, but a few days later, when I saw him on the street, he passed me without speaking. I was puzzled and hurt because I knew he had seen me. Some weeks later I met him again in public. This time he came forward with his hand extended and lifted his broad grey hat with all the gallantry of a cavalier.

"Mrs. Brown," he said softly, "I can shake hands with you now. I sold the saloon yesterday."

His face beamed as I returned the warmth of his handclasp. I realized the tribute he had paid, not to me personally, but to the wife of a respected member of a community that didn't countenance saloon-keepers, even in a frontier town.

ANY CHRONICLE OF TONOPAH should begin with the names of Tasker Oddie and Jim Butler, for they were the sparks that ignited the excitement.

It seems redundant to repeat the story of the discovery of the silver-bearing rock that made Tonopah, for today it is a routine plot for any screenplay about the discovery of a mine. The prospector travels the desert alone from one water hole to another. Failing to reach the appointed oasis before nightfall, he camps a few miles short of his destination. At daybreak he discovers his burro has wandered high up on the side of an adjacent mountain, and he picks up a rock to hurl at the animal. The rock is heavy; his arm pauses in midair. The rock looks like quartz, bearing precious metal. Of course, the prospector is penniless; in order to get the rock assayed, he must share his discovery with a friend.

Haven't you heard all this before? It has been repeated with only slight variations in settings in Montana, Arizona, New Mexico, California. But this time the narrative is not fiction. Jim Butler, owner of a few acres of homesteaded ranchland in Monitor Valley, prospector by avocation, picked up the rock on May 19, 1900, and Tasker Oddie was the friend to whom he appealed for help. Jim Butler was traveling to the next water hole from an ancient Indian oasis known as Klondike Wells — named, I judge, by some man who had been in the Alaska gold rush. Most of those way stations had some old "desert rat" living there. Butler camped about ten miles short of the water hole, known as *Tonombe,* "water near the surface." Since Butler's wife was half Shoshone, he probably used the Shoshone word *pah,* "water" when he described to Tasker Oddie the place where he made the discovery. And the name Tonopah became established for the district. The variation in the cast of characters of this mining story is the addition of the name of Belle Butler, the prospector's wife. She knew the dangers Jim faced every time he walked the desert alone: days and miles between water holes when a lame burro, a leaking canteen, a careless step into a prairie dog's hole were often the slender margin between safety and slow death.

In gratitude for Jim's survival and their good fortune, Belle Butler, a religious woman, insisted that the name of the original claim should be the "Mizpah," a word taken from the Old Testament story of Jacob and his father-in-law, who established a covenant to end the long suspicion between them. It is, in ancient Hebrew, a vow that no harm shall come to either of them through anything the other may do while they are separated. In the course of time, *mizpah* — meaning "The Lord watch between me and thee while we are absent one from another"— has come to signify the prayer of two who love each other that God will take care of them both while they are apart. In appreciation of Belle Butler, whom I never knew, Hugh and I had MIZPAH engraved in our wedding rings.

By the time I arrived in Tonopah, the Butlers had already gone to California to enjoy the fruits of their good fortune, and Tasker Oddie was for me the link between the rock that missed being hurled at a burro and the leasers who were swarming like ants over Mount Oddie.

Tasker had been sent to Nevada on a commission from the Phelps-Stokes interests in New York. They had extensive ownership in the state — land, mines, and railroads — about which they needed detailed reports. Caught by the lure of the West, Tasker, after he had completed his investigation, decided to stay in Nevada. For a few years he prospected without any luck; then, rather than return to the East, he ran for district attorney of Nye County, of which the county seat was the little town of Belmont.

Carrying a bag of specimens, Jim Butler tramped into Belmont, seventy miles beyond the spot where he had collected the rocks, in order to show them to Tasker Oddie, the only man he wanted to trust. But Tasker didn't have eight dollars to risk on an assay fee, even with Jim's promise of half interest if the rocks proved to have any value. However, in the course of the Phelps-Stokes investigations, Tasker had made a friend of Walter Gayhart, a science teacher in Austin who had a small assay outfit in his home. Tasker decided to ship the samples to his friend, offering him a percentage of his own half interest if the samples proved to be worth anything.

The stage coach trip was long and slow, and waiting for return information was hard. I heard Tasker tell of the agony it was, the cold chills he experienced when the letter did arrive. He was afraid to open it. When he did open it and began to realize the significance of the assayer's figures, he was almost afraid to accept the report as correct. But he knew Gayhart was a capable man. The promise held out by these meager samples was too exciting to be dismissed. These rocks might have come from the lost Breyfogle — the will-o'-the-wisp that had had men combing southern Nevada for forty years for the rich ore cropping that, according to legend, a prospector had staked out, then never could find again.

ASSAYS OF SAMPLES OF ORE FROM T. L. ODDIE

Sample 1	Silver 23 ounces	Gold $6.70	per ton
Sample 2	Silver 540 ounces	Gold $206.70	per ton
Sample 3	Silver 60 ounces	Gold $19.00	per ton
Sample 4	Silver 8 ounces	Gold $2.25	per ton
Sample 5	Silver 60 ounces	Gold $75.60	per ton
Sample 6	Silver 5 ounces	Gold $2.67	per ton
Sample 7	Silver 15 ounces	Gold $2.40	per ton

Jim and Tasker decided to ask Wilse Brougher to come into the partnership. Like the others, Wilse had few dollars to risk, but among the three they managed to pool twenty-five dollars. Jim had shovels and a pick, and Wilse had a small windlass and a team of horses. One moonless night they slipped out of Belmont in an old "dead-ax" wagon, as the wagons built for especially heavy loads and rough terrain were called. For three days they inched across the hot August desert. Finally Jim pointed out the pregnant spot. Only after location notices were made out and anchored down with stones did they make camp for the night. At daybreak the digging began.

"I was cook for the outfit," Tasker told me, "and I never learned to gauge the expanding power of beans. I'd make the fire and throw some beans into the pot and fill the pot to the brim with water. Then I'd climb down the hole that was getting to be a shaft, and every day I'd come back and find those dang beans swelled all over the place. All over the pot. Down into the fire. I never did learn to keep those things harnessed."

There were endless stories of flapjacks flipped onto shirt-fronts, of sour-dough biscuits and mulligan stew —"we put everything in but the soap"— of aching muscles at sundown, eased only by the thin, rich stream of values in every day's samplings.

Two tons of sacked ore, all they could safely load into the old wagon, was hauled to Belmont, then by stage to Austin. Thence, still with great secrecy, it was shipped by rail to a smelter in Salt Lake City.

For the first shipment they received $600. From that first shipment on, Tasker and his partners were in business. From the beginning to the end of the town's productive years, Tonopah produced $149,000,000.* The greater percentage of that figure came from the Tonopah Mining Company and its companion, the Belmont Development Company. These two mines comprised the original claims Tasker and his two partners staked out the day they arrived. The only development money put into these claims was the $25 in grub "risked" by the original locators.

One of the most interesting things about the Tonopah discovery was the fact that Jim Butler walked over the only spot on that mountain where the vein appeared on the surface, and the mountain was the only spot anywhere in the district where ore-bearing rocks could be found.

A discovery of precious metal is a good deal like a love affair. No matter how carefully the secret is guarded, the knowledge of it seems to fly through the air. That location was in a completely untracked desert, but a flood of prospectors began to appear as if they had sprung from the ground. They came on foot and on horseback, often without money, equipment, or food. Soon their tents and makeshift shacks spread across the valley floor, and the boom was on.

Tonopah was not immune to the rough and sometimes dangerous elements who were to be found trying to get their share of the new riches. Stories about claim-jumpers abounded. One of the best was the run-in Tasker Oddie had with Jack Longstreet, a big, powerful giant with a well-established reputation as a gunman. He had arrived in camp after all the land had been staked out, but that did not stop him from "making some locations." Then he accused Jim Clifford of jumping his claims, and followed him to Tasker's tent office on Main Street. With pistol drawn, Longstreet charged into the tent where Clifford and Oddie, both unarmed, were seated. Tasker sprang to his feet and grabbed the gun. The hammer came down on his finger, inflicting an ugly wound, but Tasker hung on and disarmed the raging man. In true western-movie style, Jack Longstreet's progress toward Tasker's tent had been reported along the street, and the sheriff arrived to take over in the nick of time.

Once many years later, I asked Tasker for the best claim-jumping tale he could remember.

"Well," he said, "I can tell you the one that meant the most to me. Some ruffians moved in from Salt Lake and tried to jump the Mizpah,

---

*For this estimate I am indebted to David Myrick, who based it on information from records at the University of Nevada. Of the total value, $24,000,000 was paid in dividends.

the original claim. Ralph Wardle and I went up on the hill to put them off and found three men down the fifteen-foot shaft. Wardle and I climbed down the ladder, and before we knew it, we were in a hand-to-hand scrap, three of them against two of us. People down in town got wind of trouble on the hill, so the sheriff rounded up some men to go up there with him. He poked his head over the edge of the shaft, looking to me like the Angel Gabriel, and yelled, 'Hey! *you* fellas got no business on this property. Quit-fightin' and get outta that hole!'

"One of them let go of me long enough to yell back, 'You can't stop us, Sheriff. You gotta have a warrant to stop us, and you can't get it. The Court House is seventy miles away in Belmont.'

"The sheriff yelled back, 'You come outta there and we'll talk about it.' By this time half the town was up on the hill. We all scrambled up the ladder.

"Then the sheriff said, 'Now I'll show you coots whether I can do something about this or not. All you fellas who are in favor of the Tonopah Mining Company's claim come over here.' About fifty men came over and stood by me.

" 'Now all you other rattlers who think these men are not thieves join up with them over there. Now, Oddie, I'll arrest anyone that comes over here from over there. You go hire a man to ride to Belmont and get out a warrant for malicious mischief, and we'll file that suit. And while you're at it, Oddie, hire enough men to keep these coyotes outta that hole. I'll stay here until you get back.' "

Tasker went on to tell me that he hired a young man who had just come into camp from Arizona. His name was Wyatt Earp. Had I ever heard about him? He was a fancy crack shot. Earp hired twenty men to help him keep the jumpers off the Mizpah claim, and Tasker paid them twenty dollars a day for six days. "That was an expensive little bit of litigation," Tasker said, "but I never spent money more effectively. It established all the Tonopah Mining Company's claims, and we never had another lawsuit."

In later years when Tasker Oddie and I talked of the early days, I realized, as I had not in my youth, how Tonopah mining differed

---

*David Myrick tells me a little item in the Tonopah Bonanza of February 1, 1902, says Wyatt Earp had come to town from Nome, and in a copy of the same paper a month later, there is an advertisement for "THE NORTHERN — Wyatt Earp, prop. A gentleman's resort." Later he returned to Arizona and became sheriff of Tombstone.

from the placer mining in California, where a man could work out a good day's wages by crouching at the edge of a stream and rolling a few pounds of dirt in a pan over which he poured an occasional swish of water. It took expensive equipment to work the underground deposits. Tasker and his partners agreed to lease ground on the vein to men who could furnish the equipment needed. Out of the many who applied, leases were let to one hundred and thirty men. The leases stipulated the percentage royalty the owners were to receive, the number of feet each lessee was entitled to (one hundred feet on the vein, fifty feet on either side), and the number of months the leases were to run.

They were negotiated without the scratch of a pen, Tasker told me, just a few brief, rough notes he made in his little memorandum book. And nobody ever lost a nickel. He said he didn't believe such a volume of complicated business was ever transacted before with so little formality. He was very proud of those leases, based as they were on confidence and good faith among many different men.

He said that by January 1, 1901, Mount Oddie was alive with the leasers. The desert was dotted with twenty-mule teams loaded with high-grade ore, making the slow journey over the sixty-five miles to Sodaville, thence by the fussy little narrow-gauge to Mound House, ultimately by Southern Pacific Railroad to the smelters in California or Colorado. As men clawed at the surface day and night, no one knew what wealth the next few feet might uncover. Every foot seemed to raise the values. Even when I came to Nevada in February of 1904, men were still working over the waste and making good returns.

But hard-rock mining needs expensive machinery to drive through rock to the veins, expert geologists to follow the veins of ore, and mills and chemists to reduce the ore to metal. The original claims were too costly for the owners to develop so they were sold outright to a group of Philadelphia investors for $336,000.

The verbal contracts with the leasers ended December 31, 1901, two months after the date of sale, but Tasker and Jim Butler insisted that all the leases were to be honored until their expiration dates. The buyers demurred but finally had to agree, and in the next two months they were paid $30,000 in royalties from the leasers. At midnight on December 31, every man who had a gun or pistol shot it off in a big celebration.

A Piano by Mule-Team ... The Fine Art of Mule-
skinning ... Dresden China in Tin-Cup Country
... Riding Breeches and "Calling" Gowns ...
A New Kind of Pioneer ... Celebrated Gunmen
and the Glamorous Redlight

ONE DAY SEVERAL WEEKS AFTER MY ARRIVAL, Hugh called on the telephone to tell me that our household belongings had come. Did I want
to come down and watch the unloading of the wagons?

I had looked forward with no little concern to the arrival of our
wedding gifts, wondering how they would survive the long trip by
mule team, so it didn't take me long to change my dress and skip down
the hill. The freight station was behind the Merchant's Hotel, almost
in the center of town, and I had to elbow my way through a crowd of
miners, Indians and general idlers. The pack train consisted of at least
four freight wagons hitched together, each piled high with mining
machinery, supplies, furniture, barrels, and — my piano!

As I reached the freight station the "muleskinner" had already un-
hitched his string of seventeen mules and three horses, and was leading
the horses away. I gazed at him in amazement. Every inch of that man
was coated with a fine layer of dust; every individual hair stood out.
His eyes peering from under eyelashes heavy with desert "mascara,"
his powdered face with the inevitable tobacco lines around the mouth
looked as if he had been made up for a grotesque harlequinade.

I didn't laugh, though I wanted to. I hadn't been on the frontier long,
but long enough to know I was in the presence of royalty. No men had
greater dignity or more right to pride than the men who maneuvered
the wagon trains over the mountains and up the dry canyons of Nevada.

For a time I just stood watching him in the corral. Carefully he
watered his horses; then he fed them. But he ignored the mules. I
wondered why and, unable to find an acquaintance in the crowd to
ask, I inquired from a stranger why he devoted all his time to the
horses. Didn't the mules deserve some attention?

The man looked at me as if I didn't have good sense. "Mules are
mules," he mumbled. "Any roustabout can take care of them. But
horses are partners."

I didn't dare ask any more questions, but I was so intrigued by his
reply that later I repeated it to William Blackburn, the superintendent
of the Tonopah Mining Company. He understood my puzzlement. It
seems everything on a mule train depends upon a nice understanding

between the man and his three horses. The lead horse especially has to have real "horse sense." Fastened to his bridle is a jerk line, running along the harness to the driver's hand forty feet or more away, the distance depending on the number of mules between the lead horse and the wheelers. The lead horse must respond correctly when the driver pulls the jerk line, once for a left turn and twice for a right. What is more, that horse must know to a foot how far to circle out on a turn so that the mules jump the slack chain at just the right distance to ease the wagons safely around the bend. More than once in after-years I saw this maneuver, and it is really something beautiful to see. The lead horse swings far out to left or right, as the case may be, and the mules jump the chain in rhythm — like a swimming team jumping into the water one after another.

But even more responsible are the wheel horses. The wheelers control the strains on a freight wagon. When a wagon is properly loaded, with the weight of the cargo concentrated over the back axle, brakes will hold under any kind of road conditions. But there is a moment, as the brakes are released, when the wheelers must be depended on to hold back the weight of the wagon, easing it off slowly, just enough so that the mules can take on the weight without getting fouled up in the slack chain. As the man said, "On a wagon train horses are 'partners' on a hazardous journey," Mr. Blackburn concluded.

Ultimately the stablemen did come along to care for the mules, and by the time all the animals were standing with heads down and one foot at parade rest, the muleskinner was well on his way uptown to his favorite saloon. What with drinks for the house and money for the girl friend, before morning he would probably be broke again.

Now the freight-handlers began climbing on the wagons, slowly unscrambling the freight. I saw our barrels lowered casually to the ground and piled together. Oh, my beautiful china! Then came the piano, with a sickening jolt. I wondered what the jar would do to it, not to mention the awful impregnation of dust from the journey. Later, to my delight, I found that it was not hurt.

We spent exciting days unpacking, wondering all the while where in the tiny house we were going to stow everything. Of course, most of what we received as wedding gifts was fit only for a city home. Our friends were no more prepared for the conditions we were to meet than I was myself. But the cut glass, the Dresden china, the beautiful linen and silver all contributed to our gaiety, even if the environment did seem to call for oilcloth and tin cups.

One of the handsomest gifts we received was a large bronze kerosene lamp from Judge Jackson and his wife. The shade was a huge red glass globe. Handsome as it was, in our tiny box of a house the lamp was like a Newfoundland pup in a doll's house.

As the little group of intimate friends gravitated more and more to our house, we seemed to laugh louder and play harder in our two-by-four living room than anywhere else in town. One night the beautiful bronze lamp was tipped over, and the big red globe went hurtling through the window glass with a noise like a pistol shot.

For a moment we were silent with dismay, but youth is resilient, and soon we were laughing again. However, the next morning I gave myself over to tears as the poor bronze lamp, its beautiful shade gone and its wick hanging out like a dry tongue, was banished to the dugout we used as a cellar. It remained in the dugout storage for as long as we lived in Tonopah. Years afterward, when we returned to California, I arranged to have the lamp converted to an electric fixture. To my surprise the gentleman with whom I dealt raved over it.

It was the color and luster of the metal that impressed him. When I told him the history of the lamp, he said that it was possible the bronze had absorbed chemicals from its long contact with Tonopah's metal-impregnated earth, and that might account for its unusual luster.

My trousseau was as inappropriate to Boomtown as my wedding presents, but at the time it didn't seem so. We all dressed with the same care we would have used in any established community. My "calling dress" was a lovely shade of purple velvet, trimmed with an exquisite "fancy" of marabou. My traveling suit, a thin broadcloth we called "lady's cloth," was made with a short Eton jacket lined with white silk. I wore with it the red poppy hat that caught Hugh's eye at Hawthorne. The skirt was daringly short — four inches off the ground.

The day Mrs. Hank Knight called, she had said to me playfully, "Well, Mrs. Brown, it is all very well for you to arrive here with your stylish frou-frous, but you wait. The time will come when you'll go back to San Francisco, and you'll walk up Market Street feeling just as dowdy as we do."

When women in California took to driving automobiles in riding breeches and short coats, I wore them in Tonopah and was very seriously criticized by other women. But I don't think the men minded. I had an echo of this many years later, when an old friend I hadn't seen since Tonopah days said to me, "Marjorie, you don't look natural to me. I remember you in dark grey riding togs with black boots up to your knees and a saucy black hat. You looked like a handsome boy."

Of course we would dress much more sensibly now, but in 1904, we brought to the desert the scale of living to which we were born. To dress the part of the frontiersman just wasn't done. Those who attempted it were considered show-offs. For the most part, Tonopah was a community of city people who lived in rough-board houses and walked unpaved streets, but who dressed and acted as they would in San Francisco or New York.

I have had occasion to read the experiences of an English woman who visited Colorado in 1875. She traveled by horseback from Truckee in California, across the Great Divide to Estes Park, in Colorado. Her account of the pioneers of that day interested me greatly, for I was impressed with the fact that by 1900 the Buffalo Bill variety of show-off, as well as the "murder for breakfast every day" badmen, was out of date.

When men who never saw Tonopah write of this period, stressing the gun-toting adventurer, they are drawing a long bow. To be sure, the gunman, the dance-hall girl, and the gambler were all realities, but the lawlessness was over. When my husband and I were young, another kind of pioneer had emerged — the geologist, the mining engineer, the chemist, the lawyer, men whose grubstake was a college diploma. They lived on the frontier, but they were not the fictional version of frontiersmen.

However, we were not without our flamboyant characters, who might be described as a link between the old, lawless West and the modern community, where productivity depended on law and order. One such character was cattleman and politician John Sparks, who came from Texas to Nevada sometime in the '80s. He brought with him not only his Longhorns and Herefords, but also his gunman, Jack Davis, who knew the technique of border raiding.

Sparks had some grazing land up north in Nevada close to the Idaho line. There was a man over in Idaho he suspected of encroaching on grazing land he considered as his own, so he sent Jack Davis over into Idaho to kill him. Jack succeeded, but before he got back across the state line into Nevada he was captured by an Idaho sheriff, tried, and condemned to death. John Sparks had influence enough over there to get Davis' execution delayed three times. Then, in 1903, Sparks was elected governor of Nevada. The first thing he did was to appeal to his friend the governor of Idaho to pardon the gunman — which he promptly did.

In Tonopah January Jones and Bar Francis were also referred to as gun-toters, and they carried their weapons more or less openly. The butt of January's bulged just below his right shoulder blade. I couldn't figure out what would happen if he ever had to draw that weapon in a hurry. It looked to me as if he would have to reach down his collar. I don't think he was much of a fighter and may have worn his pistol in a way that would make it hard to pull. Although he looked like a brigand and had the reputation of having more than one notch to his credit, January was a peaceful, law-abiding citizen in Tonopah, married to the lady barber and altogether respectable.

Bar Francis was a man of similar appearance and somewhat the same reputation. In later years, upon reading Eleanor Roosevelt's book, *This I Remember,* I was startled to run across the name of Bar Francis. In the chapter headed "The Peaceful Years," she mentions visiting the ranch of Mr. and Mrs. Dana near Reno where "the caretaker of the horses was a wonderful old character named Bar Francis, who had been an old-time badman and later sheriff." I don't think Bar Francis was ever a western badman in the accepted meaning of the term, but I am sure he enjoyed the reputation.

Harry Ramsey, whom I had first met on the stage for Tonopah, was another of the quiet, inconspicuous, soft-spoken men who for that very reason carried the unsavory reputation of killer. If rumors were facts, his gun had nine notches on it, acquired in Mexico when he cleaned out a nest of bandits who had killed his father and brother. This hardly seemed to justify labeling him a "western" killer, but he did carry that reputation: deliberate, calm, and absolutely ruthless.

And what of the glamorous ladies from the other end of town? Occasional tales filtered through to me — I wish I had known more; it would have been livelier for this book if I had. There were a few, not the usual dance-hall girls, who achieved a certain amount of notoriety, if not fame, as they moved from one lucky gambler to another when the turn of fortune swung high or low. Wearing a touch of rouge in an era when makeup was a *sign,* they tripped across the street with long skirts held tight and hats loaded with plumes, often with parasols slung negligently over a plump shoulder. This type of young woman did not live in the redlight; I never knew where they did live.

In my day no one ever saw dance-hall girls in short, fluffy skirts, dancing the Can Can on the stage, at least not in Nevada. I did get an occasional surreptitious glimpse of the underworld. Hugh's office was in the Golden Block, diagonally opposite the famous Butler Saloon, the first saloon in camp, which boasted that its doors had never been shut. In summer the short swinging doors made it possible from Hugh's windows to see into the saloon, when the women stood at the bar, foot on rail, with the men. I was tremendously intrigued, much to my husband's disgust. "What are you so curious about?" he would say. "They're a dime a dozen. They're not even good-looking." But that wasn't always true. Sometimes they were very glamorous.

Then there were the "madams," rulers of the redlight. I can tell you two good stories about them.

One ran a house — I'll wager it was known as the Bijou or the Sagebrush or the Golden Nugget — in which no girl was allowed to rob a man. One day she discovered a certificate for ten thousand shares of Mohawk in the possession of one of the girls. The girl insisted the stock had been given to her, and maybe it was, but the madam thought differently. She cuffed the girl a bit just to teach her a lesson and then put on her hat and went uptown to find the man who owned the certificate. Stock registrations meant little in those days. All she had to do was to drop into a broker's office and sell the certificate. At that time Mohawk was worth about five dollars a share. She would have been comfortable for the rest of her life. But true to her code, she handed over the stock to the owner, who had come to her place dead-drunk. He was still drunk and hadn't yet discovered his loss. The story flew like a summer shower to revive everybody's faith in human nature.

Another woman fell in love with a gambler and wanted a child by him. She had a very well-built and roomy house down on Oddie Avenue. (Ironically one of the worst streets in town was named for our first citizen.) So the gambler married her, and the house was picked up, perched crazily on Harry Hudson's freight wagon, behind a ten-mule team, and teetered up Main Street to the farthest end of town, where it was deposited on a nice flat piece of ground. Here, a few months later, her baby was born as far from the redlight as she could get — and legitimate.

One day I heard a dirge being played downtown on Main Street, and I wondered who had died that was important enough to turn out the Miners' Union Band. I telephoned to Hugh, and he told me that it was a girl from the redlight. She had always wanted a wedding gown, it was said, so her friends bought her a white satin wedding dress, veil and all, and laid her out in it. They held the funeral in the Miners' Union Hall, and the hearse followed the band down to the graveyard.

There was another kind of woman — wife to no man and far from the sporting world — who played the hard game like the men. These women went to every new strike, put up their own location notices, and dug their own assessment holes. When Lady Luck looked the other way, they ran boarding houses for the miners, which was not too easy a life either. Occasionally, they were large, burly women, but more often they were thin and wiry. One wondered how they were able to survive the fierce living they faced.

While I am on this subject, I want to say I love a good western movie. The brilliant fireflies, the rough saloons, the unpaved streets, the riding cowboys, the gun-toting gamblers, and the brave marshals — jazzed up but still recognizable — are characters right out of my own experience. The sound of the bell on the toy engines pulling into way-stations at night can bring tears to my eyes, because I know it is quite possible I am seeing again the same little engine and listening to the same sweet sound that accompanied me into Sodaville on my wedding journey.

Not all our men were tailored in grey wool or gabardine. We had one real Tonopah pioneer who did wear flannel shirts. He was the leaser. Again, he was a different kind of man from those who panned California gold in Grass Valley or climbed icy Chilkoot Pass in the Klondike rush of '98. Young and pretty well-educated, he was stalwart enough to handle a drill or swing a ten-pound hammer. Leasers were a tough breed, and not too proud for "mucking"— that is, clearing out the debris after a dynamite blast with a shovel, or "muck-stick."

In eighteen months the leasers — perhaps 160 men — produced four million dollars for themselves. When the surface deposits had been worked out and the waste dumps worked over, these young leasers could no longer function. After that, Tonopah settled down to a steady growth under the management of eastern capitalists, who hired an army of specialists to sink deep shafts, trace rich veins out into unknown territory, and reduce ore-bearing rock to bullion.

Typical of the men who made fortunes out of the leasing system was Tom Lynch, and his marriage to May Edwards, a tall, handsome blonde, was not only a social highlight, but it dramatized the leasing period. Tom knew everyone, and the invitation to his wedding reception was published in the Tonopah Bonanza. Dress suits and gowns from Paris rubbed shoulders with business suits and clean khaki. Opera hats and ostrich plumes mingled with wide Stetsons and miners' caps.

I remember well what I wore that night: a semi-evening dress of heavy black silk, trimmed with smocking around the waist and down over the hips, very flattering to the Gibsonesque hourglass figure of the day. The hat I wore with it was a creation of black lace with two long black ostrich feathers curling down directly back of my left ear.

Tom's house, up on the hill very close to our own, had been transformed from a little four-roomed shack into an irregular but spacious home of eight rambling rooms. The wedding was held in the Catholic Church, and the reception was at their home. On the dining table was a big punch bowl into which two men poured champagne, while two others rapidly ladled it into glasses, which were emptied and refilled as fast as hands could move. The crowd milled up to the table and away, a continual churning for hours.

Every possible space in that house was covered with wedding presents. My little house was bulging with my own wedding presents, and they weren't a tenth of what had been sent to this bride. What could the new Mrs. Lynch do with this flood of gifts I often wondered.

After the reception our little coterie decided to end the evening at our house. Hugh came trudging up the hill a little late, his arms stacked high with bottles of champagne. I was furious. We had had all the champagne that was good for us. Turning to him with great dignity, I said, "You shouldn't have done it! I don't want anyone to go from my house tipsy away." With a roar that shook the little house, the bottles were dragged from Hugh's arms and opened, corks popping like a toy pistol barrage.

I never did live down that speech. Every once in a while, even today, someone reminds me that no one must ever go from my house tipsy away.

*Our Friend Tasker . . . Introducing the Oddie Family
. . . The "Damn Horse" Rondo . . . Pine Creek Ranch
. . . Dancing, 300 Feet Underground . . . A Guided Tour
through the Tunnels . . . The Glory Hole, "Sweetest
Ground in the District". . . Six Inches from Perfection*

WHEN I ARRIVED IN TONOPAH, Tasker Oddie was in New York nego-
tiating the sale of some of the claims owned by him and his partners.
He was by no means unknown to me, however, for Hugh's letters had
set the stage of Tonopah with Tasker as the hero.

I met him, of course, as soon as he returned. He was a tall man, over
thirty and somewhat bald, on the crest of a wave of good fortune, gay
and generous.

From the moment Hugh had arrived in camp, almost a year earlier,
these two men had been comrades. Both were graduate lawyers, Hugh
from Stanford, Tasker from New York University; both had been selected because of character and attainments to go to the frontier on errands
of trust; both were typical twentieth century pioneers. Tasker was the
outdoor man, bronzed, khaki-clad, with high-laced boots and broad-
brimmed Stetson; Hugh, the office man, the counsellor, equally tall
and slender but clothed in the same grey suits and white collars he
wore in San Francisco — except for a battered old grey hat.

"This hat? Why, this hat is the concession I make to my environment."

In 1904 Tasker was grading the roadbed on the flat west of town for
the railroad that was slowly approaching us. He had brought in some
fifty draft horses to do the job, and a few saddle horses, among them
Rondo, his special mount, together with a magnificent pair of trotters
he maintained for traveling to Sodaville, where he met the Southern
Pacific. We rode horseback with him almost every Sunday, ending
with supper at his home or ours. There was little in the way of entertainment outside our homes and Tasker's horses added variety and
great pleasure to our lives.

Like a silver thread through our lives ran our friendship with the
Oddie family. Tasker's mother and sisters came to Tonopah after the
silver strike, and the youngest sister, Anna, married Fred Siebert, a
promising mining engineer, soon after their arrival. They were a
magnificent-looking pair. All the Oddies were tall, but Anna was the
tallest of the three girls —"just under six feet with my shoes off," she
told me — and Fred topped her by four inches. Anna and I established
a friendship that lasted throughout our lives. As long as Tasker kept

horses in Tonopah, we rode together, and later our children played together.

The Oddies were a high-spirited family. Of the five brothers and sisters, Sarah was the most striking — tall and slender, with large capable hands, unruly red-blonde hair, and a wide smile disclosing firm white teeth. An able horsewoman, as all the sisters were, she was particularly at home in the saddle. My most vivid recollection of Sarah is riding "Bill Nye," a black Thoroughbred that snorted and cavorted and danced himself into a lather. Sarah managed him with courage, plainly enjoying the excitement, for he was just dangerous enough to demand all the skill she possessed.

Speaking of the Oddie horses reminds me of an incident with Tasker and Rondo. I happened to be at the upper end of town on the road leading to a location called "The Divide" when I heard a horse galloping toward me. It was Rondo, covered with foam, clattering over the hill, Tasker up, face red and eyes blazing. As he drew rein in front of me, he shouted, "This damn horse tried to kill me! He tried to scrape me off that building. This time I wore him down. I ran him clear out to the Divide and back."

I called, "You both look as if you had been through a battle." But I don't think he heard me with Rondo snorting so.

"He's wicked! Meanest brute I ever owned," Tasker yelled as they danced away. And you love him for his wickedness, I thought, as I watched them disappear. Rondo was Tasker's favorite among all his saddle horses, but every moment he was on that animal's back was a struggle for mastery. Rondo was a true challenge to his master's magnificent horsemanship.

Tasker's fortune continued to grow for a number of years, for his interests were scattered all over southern Nevada, but his heart was centered in a huge ranch in Monitor Valley some sixty miles east of Tonopah.

Pine Creek Ranch was ten thousand acres of beautiful grazing land stocked with blooded cattle, by means of which Tasker planned to raise the standard of livestock throughout the state. His prize Hereford bull was the noblest animal I ever saw.

We all loved to be invited to Pine Creek, for Tasker was a delightful host indeed. As long as the weather would permit, eight months in the year, the rambling ranch house bulged with company, Nevadans and easterners. Literally, we ate off the fat of the land, rode horseback over the lovely countryside, and sat on the wide porch of the ranch house watching the Herefords roam the hills, while the lights and shadows of desert sunlight made pictures in pastel. The year Halley's Comet made its appearance, we were at Pine Creek, and all got up at four o'clock in the morning to watch it go trailing across the clear desert sky — a celestial pony tail.

Most of our social life revolved around the Oddies. Tasker lived near us on the edge of Mount Brougher in a house that started out as a cabin, but had been remodeled in anticipation of the visit by his mother and sisters. It became a big, rambling dwelling of two large main rooms at right angles, with bedrooms strung around wherever they could be attached without shutting off the light. Tasker's Chinese servant, who went by the name of Charlie Oddie, was a marvelous cook and produced the most delectable things out of cans. Of course, Tasker imported all sorts of delicacies: oysters, fruit, vegetables, candies, perishables packed in ice and transported at tremendous cost three days from San Francisco. You had to be a potential millionaire to indulge in such extravagances.

In a mining camp, underground developments are always more exciting than anything that happens on the surface, and I was very anxious to go down one of the mines. Finally, the opportunity came with a mysterious invitation from Tasker. We were instructed to assemble at the "Oddie Mansion" at nine o'clock in the evening on a given date. The card read, "Wear your digging clothes." When we had all gathered at Tasker's house, one of his big dirt wagons pulled up in front. Boards had been laid across sawhorses for seats, and about twenty of us piled in.

I was motioned to climb up with the driver, so I scrambled up over the giant wheel from one of the spokes to the rim. Then grabbing hold of the long brake, I managed to pull myself up to the seat beside the driver with *no help*. As we started down Mount Brougher, the horses strained back in the traces to keep from plunging too fast down the steep grade. The driver had his hands full. As for me, up there above the team with nothing to hold on to except the thin rod around the seat, the ride was quite terrifying but exhilarating. Once off the hill, we jangled merrily across town and up Mount Oddie to the Mizpah mine.

The mine shaft was really theatrical. The headframe was lighted by brilliant flood lights; even the engine room sent out a pool of brightness. The lights reflecting on the surrounding country made the buildings appear to be set in snow, for the ground is gray, and the desert

*My portrait in 1906,
when the boom seemed
destined to last forever.*

*Hugh in 1906.
His legal fees were often
paid in mining stock and leases.*

*Taken the day after our
wedding. A few hours later
we left for Tonopah—via
three rail lines and a
jouncing stagecoach.*

Tonopah, 1901: population, 900. The bewhiskered gentleman under the derby is C. W. Ingalls, correspondent for the Mining and Scientific Press, San Francisco. At his feet lies the rich Mizpah ledge.

Main Street, 1903. Until the railroad arrived the next year, all freight bound for Tonopah had to come in wagons like this one —often pulled over the mountains by twenty-mule teams.

Water wagons. That precious desert commodity was delivered to our door each week. The wagon driver had to carry it bucket by bucket to the big barrel in our kitchen.

An early street scene. In spite of boardwalks and dusty roads, most people dressed as they would in Chicago or San Francisco.

"Sodaville and Tonopah Stage Office. J. O'Keefe, Prop."
Hugh's law office was on the second floor
of the new Golden Block next door.

Customers of Ryan & Stenson, 1902.

In treeless Tonopah building a house took imagination. The first year, miners used barrels, packing boxes, tin cans, gunny sacks, even the desert earth itself.

The Mizpah mine shaft. From left: a promoter named Jenkins; Jim Butler, who made the first strike at Tonopah; his wife Belle, who gave the claim its biblical name; the ubiquitous newsman C. W. Ingalls; several of the Mizpah miners; and at far right, Tasker Oddie, future governor of Nevada.

Tasker Oddie, Jenkins, and Mr. and Mrs. Butler. On the horizon, just to the right of the stovepipe, is the pile of rocks Jim Butler erected to mark the original Mizpah claim.

Main Street, looking toward Goldfield. That first winter of the boom (1901-02), a pneumonia epidemic took fifty lives.

night is never quite black. The big cage carried us underground in groups of six. As we dropped down on silent cables, the smell of deep earth came up to meet us, and the strong wind blowing past made the air cold. Suddenly the cage emerged into a spot of blazing lights and came to a gradual stop.

We stepped out at the station on the three-hundred-foot level. It was a huge excavation about thirty feet square and fully that high, floored with heavy steel plates on which the ore cars were shifted, when empty, into the tunnels extending unlighted in three directions away from the shaft. When the ore cars returned filled, they were maneuvered into the cage and hoisted to the surface. The constant scraping and turning of the cars had polished the steel plates to a high gloss.

That night we had a dancing party three hundred feet underground on the smooth steel floor. What a unique event! The music? Three miners playing two accordions and a banjo, with muted sounds of pounding hammers and rolling ore cars adding an obbligato from mysterious distances, whence men with candles on their caps appeared and disappeared like giant lightning bugs. At ten o'clock our revelry was stopped by a sudden sensation, a feeling that our bodies were being pressed in from all sides at once. Then someone turned the electric light off, and we were in darkness.

We knew that dynamite was being exploded on the levels below us, and that all candles had been snuffed out by the concussion. An atmosphere of unmistakable tension filled the darkness while nine shots were detonated. When the lights were restored, Hugh told me how serious it was for every shot to be recorded, since only eight shots would mean that a hole had missed firing. It would have to be discovered and unloaded before the next shift of miners arrived, so that no one would face the hazard of sudden death by striking a pick into the missed hole.

Then we had supper: cold chicken, salad, and sandwiches brought in great hampers from the Oddie home, with hot coffee lowered to us down the shaft from the miners' bunkhouse on the surface. After supper, Tasker took me for a tour of the mine. This was old stuff to the rest of the party, but I was eager to explore.

He stuffed a short candle into a miner's candlestick for me. Then, holding his own candle over his head so that the wavering light would guide me as I stumbled along behind him, he led the way about a hundred feet through one of the tunnels. In a few moments we came out into a vast subterranean excavation, crossed and recrossed overhead with a forest of logs a foot in diameter.

"Now this," Tasker began, "is the sweetest piece of ground in the district." Then he went on to explain that this rich pocket of high-grade ore had been mined out all the way to the surface, a distance of three hundred feet; that every ounce of metal-bearing rock on the vein had been drilled out, leaving the non-bearing rock as smooth as a wall on both sides. And every ounce was high-grade, that is richer than average ore.

He held the candle aloft so that the soft light would penetrate the forest of logs overhead. "Do you mean this whole excavation was high-grade?" I asked.

"That's right. We call this stope the 'Glory Hole.' Thousands of tons of rock have been mined out from this space, and every ton was high-grade straight up to the grass roots."

I knew the shipments were standardized to hundred-dollar ore, a bit of information I had gleaned elsewhere. Tasker went on to say that some of the ore ran as high as a thousand dollars a ton. But the values all over the mine were not so high, so they sweetened from the Glory Hole. Every time a shipment fell below a hundred dollars a ton, they put in a few tons from there and the values would reach the required level.

To look aloft and try to visualize the amount of money this great excavation represented dramatized for me the magnitude of the Tonopah discovery. Discussions with my father during the months I was engaged helped me evaluate what I was seeing now. Because I was going to a mining camp to live, he thought I should understand the worldwide importance of the discovery of gold and silver in Nevada. Only a few years before, the United States had emerged from the Spanish-American War in dire need of gold. Men who might have been prospectors were instead becoming homesteaders on free land in the West, and as a result, the discovery of precious metals had been practically nil for years. Now, millions of dollars were pouring into the economy of the nation in a beneficent stream.

Conversations with geologists and mining engineers had aroused in me an interest in the developments of the mines themselves, an interest that never flagged. This was something I could more readily understand than the economics of new money.

As we passed a certain point on our return to the station platform, Tasker pointed to a spot where a right-angle jog appeared on both sides of the tunnel, the testimonial, he said, of an engineer's job well done.

He held his candle against the side wall so that I might examine the little six-inch shift in alignment. He saw me looking a bit lost, so he explained that there were two shafts at the Mizpah. The first one was sunk about a hundred feet from where he and Jim Butler dug the location hole. Next, they put down another shaft on the Desert Queen claim and connected the two shafts on this level. They crosscut each of these shafts to meet at a determined point three hundred feet below the surface, as nearly at right angles to the shaft as possible so that the floor of the tunnel would be level. And that six-inch jog was how close the engineer had come to perfect alignment.

I was much impressed. To my ignorance, it seemed fantastic that men could drill down into the earth for three hundred feet in two shafts separated by a quarter of a mile, strike out seemingly blind, and meet at some unknown point, at direct right angles to both shafts and at the same level. This was my first acquaintance with the precision of surveyors' computations.

The mining engineer was Fred Siebert, who married Tasker's youngest sister, Anna. "We wouldn't let the men smooth off the face of that wall," Tasker said. "We told them to cut it square so that all the young bucks going to mining school who come up here on vacation can see what a veteran can do."

I'm sure Fred Siebert looked at this graphic proof of his skill with pardonable pride. Hugh told me Tasker had met Fred Siebert, as he had met Walter Gayhart, on the Phelps-Stokes assignment. When the strike was made at Tonopah, he sent for Fred to help him develop the Mizpah. Anna and Fred Siebert fell in love when Tasker's mother and sisters came west to visit him.

Women in Tonopah . . . Desert Housekeeping . . . The
Great Laundry Fiasco . . . Indian Annie's Father . . .
Banquet on Oilcloth . . . The Wonder of Ruby Silver
. . . Shakespeare and a Dogfight . . . "The Nevergreen
Tree". . . Concert, in Miner's Boots and Organdy

WHEN MY THOUGHTS RETURN to the women of Tonopah, I recall how my sympathy went out to the brides. As soon as a young man made a stake, he invariably went back for the girl he had left behind. Many were entirely unfitted for the life of a mining camp. The older women, wives of engineers, mine officials, and tradesmen, seemed adequate, but you could almost tell by looking at the brides whether they would be able to stick it out.

The problems of housekeeping on the desert were very real. During the bitter cold winters the wind moaned and whistled through the cracks in the board-and-batten houses. In the terrific summer heat, you had to cook over a wood stove with one eye always watchful for insects. Have you ever inadvertently crushed a stink bug and lived with that stench for days? Have you ever turned suddenly to look at your baby on the floor and found a scorpion on his arm? Have you ever found a bedbug on your pillow and faced the task of getting rid of the pests? The women used to say it was no disgrace to get bedbugs, but it was certainly a disgrace to keep them.

We were successors to that wonderful race of pioneer women who have been scattered over the West since the western trek began, women who brought their babies into the world in lonely places, women who cooked for their sick neighbors. These were women who washed the dead and laid them out, and rode horseback for miles to help a beleaguered home.

Jen Stock and her mother belonged to that race of women. Jen became my most intimate friend. She had a keen mind and a grand sense of humor. She did much to smooth that first year when I wrestled with new problems. She taught me to darn, to make soap, to wet paper and sprinkle the bits over the floor before I swept so that the fine talc-like dust would be kept down; and best of all, she taught me to make bread. But there was one thing she didn't teach me. She didn't teach me how to wash clothes, because I was ashamed to confess my ignorance to my more experienced neighbor.

Once I had called in Annie, an Indian woman, who looked a thousand years old though she was probably not as old as my own mother, but things were in such disorder by the time she was through that I could not think of having her in my neat little kitchen again. I watched Jen and other neighbors hang out sheets, tablecloths, pajamas, shirts, until every bit of linen I owned had been used up in an effort to postpone the evil day. At last I tackled it. If other women could do the washing, I could.

The water, remember, was in a big barrel in the kitchen. Once a week a man came up the hill behind a team of mules struggling against the weight of a wagon loaded with six huge barrels full of water. He'd stop as close to the front of the house as the uneven ground would allow, prop the back wheels with a wooden wedge, and empty one of the barrels through a bunghole into buckets. Then he came teetering into my kitchen, carrying two buckets at a time, from which water spilled across the floor, but ultimately most went into my barrel. Each week I paid him a silver dollar.

Every bit of water we used was lifted out of that barrel. Bathing was not too difficult, for we had two oversize tea kettles. One of these, heated to boiling, then poured into the big galvanized iron tub on the floor and cooled with more water, was not too hard to handle. But for laundering I had to lift the kettle from the stove to a tub balanced between two kitchen chairs, scrub the clothes as I had seen Annie do, then dip the water out with a pitcher until the tub was light enough to drag along the floor and empty out the back door. I repeated the filling process to rinse the wet, heavy sheets, not to mention the terrific effort of getting them hung on the line, and then mopped up the water that had splashed on the floor! This was more than I had ever bargained for.

The task was not half complete before I had rubbed the skin off the backs of my fingers, and when the job was done, my body ached in every joint.

When Hugh came home, I cried in his arms. Poor man, he didn't know what to do with me; but that night, when I lay in bed, my hands throbbing with pain, I made a vow: I would never try it again! Tomorrow I'd go down to the little cubbyhole on Main Street that passed for a dry goods store and buy bed linen. My husband (as if it were his fault) would have to get his shirts washed in the same way he had managed before I arrived, and everything else would go to a Reno laundry and back by stage.

Reno was two hundred miles away. It took two days for the laundry to get there and a little less than three weeks for it to return, but I've never been ashamed to confess I didn't do my washing myself. After I maneuvered Hugh into carrying the package down to the stage office, he decided to send his own linen to Reno, too. For the next two years the arrangement was a great comfort to both of us.

Washing my windows was the next source of humiliation for me though without quite serious repercussions. I had been reared by a Victorian mother who insisted that no lady should ever be seen doing menial labor. I had no hesitancy about doing the necessary scrubbing and polishing indoors — in fact I loved it — but it did give me a sense of degradation to realize I would have to go out on the porch in full sight of the whole town to wash those windows. Should I hire old Annie? Unthinkable. I'd have to do it.

So I went at it, making myself as small as possible and hoping no one would notice me. But alas for foolish wishes, that afternoon a lady knocked at the door. She was the wife of the bank cashier, and, I had been told, the granddaughter of a Virginia City millionaire. That day she was elegantly dressed in soft brown wool under a sealskin coat.

"Oh, Mrs. Brown," she announced gaily, "I've wanted to come to see you ever since you arrived, and when I saw you out washing your windows this morning, I said to myself, "There now, I'll go this very afternoon.""

I'm sure she washed her own windows, and I was relieved to think she didn't know how mortified I was. But gradually I learned it was not the doing of the menial labor that was "déclassé," but the *not* doing it. I learned to discount the toll of my complexion and the awful things that happened to my fingernails (Hugh never did get over regretting the condition of my hands), and never since have I been able to recapture the importance of such things. There is very little in the way of physical labor I haven't done, even chopping wood for the cook stove. I *love* to swing an ax!

Two more incidents of emotional impact come to mind. One was the sight of what I thought was an oriole.* There are almost no birds on the southern Nevada desert, yet here he was, perched on the uncertain branch of a sagebrush. Where had he come from? Where would he go to find a drink? I had wept a little alone in the house, for I missed my mother's affection, but the sight of that beautiful black and yellow bird triggered my first real battle with homesickness.

---

*I have since been told that it was undoubtedly a woodpecker I saw. They do get through to the desert occasionally.

On another occasion, as I was washing my breakfast dishes, there was a faint tapping at the window. I looked up and was startled by the sight of an old Indian woman peering through the glass, cupping out the light from little sunken eyes with hands that looked like bird claws. Straggling wisps of grey hair hung down from a dirty headband. She opened her mouth and poked a brown finger into a toothless black hole. I realized she was telling me she was hungry, so I fixed some food on a plate and gave it to her at the back door. It was a frightening and depressing experience, and I'm sure I knew all the paralyzing fear early settlers must have felt when they looked up to find hostile Indians at their windows.

"Pooty good eat," she said, as she handed back the empty plate and dragged herself to her feet by the stick she carried. My back window became a regular port of call for her, and I became really fond of the innocent old creature.

Speaking of hostile Indians reminds me of Annie's father. He sat on the hillside behind my house, for his daughter worked for my neighbors, and she would bring the old man along every day, taking bits of food to him at noon and at sundown. Then, when evening came, the two would trudge off to the Indian camp around the edge of the mountain.

He was a handsome old man, remarkably tall and straight for one so old, with long, thick grey hair, and he carried himself with a natural dignity. But what set him apart from other Indians were his white full-dress shirts — which he wore with the boiled bosoms in the back. Evidently they appealed to his sense of distinction. His trousers might be anything, but Annie saw to it that his shirts were snow white and meticulously ironed.

This old fellow was one of the few Indians still alive who had traveled southern Nevada on the warpath. Many of us picked up arrowheads around our own houses. I have one, the point of which is drilled with a tiny hole, and the hole has a sinister looking red stain around it. The presence of this aged Paiute chief sitting behind my house, together with poison arrowheads, made the Old West seem very close, as indeed it was.

According to accepted custom, when the old man died, the Indians burned the whole camp, a huge conglomeration of wickiups and refuse that made a barbaric blaze. For three days they covered their faces with ashes and sat on the ground in circles, wailing and chanting the old chief's spirit across the "Great Divide."

To add novelty to our lives in "boomtown," we had frequent social events, often patterned as nearly as possible after the lives we had left behind.

An early occasion in our personal experience was a dinner given by one of Hugh's clients, Mr. Charles E. Knox, president of the Montana-Tonopah Mining Company. The dinner was held in the Merchants' Hotel, a rambling, rough-board rooming house with a second-floor porch, located on lower Main Street near the corral where the freight wagons were unloaded. "No finer chef in the world," proclaimed the friends of Tom Arden, one of the proprietors, who was known to miners from the Arctic Circle to Cape Town. We dined in an inside room twenty feet long and half as wide, papered with a big sprawling design in magenta profusely ornamented with gold, and lighted by two electric bulbs suspended on cords from the ceiling. The dining table was fashioned from smaller tables pushed together, covered with white oilcloth and decorated with a centerpiece of three cactus plants in tin cans. The water glasses were beer mugs, and the coffee cups were not exactly eggshell thin; but thanks to a princely host, we were served a fruit cocktail of fresh strawberries. Tasker wasn't the only man in town who could offer his guests fruit two days by train and one day by stage from California.

The eighteen guests included men connected with the executive end of the mining interests and several wives. At each lady's place we discovered a small, flat globule of pure silver. I had to be told this was an assayer's button, the result of a test for ore values, made by the assayer in an office retort, before a shipment of ore is sent to the smelter.

These original little mementos, made from high-grade ore from the Montana-Tonopah, were not all that made the dinner memorable. Seated at Mr. Knox's right, I heard from the other end of the table bursts of unguarded laughter, with Hugh's voice in animated and continuous narrative. I had known Hugh as a man of quiet dignity, but now under the beneficent influence of the champagne, in which he had not often indulged, my husband blossomed out as a raconteur.

Another trip underground was arranged for me by Mr. Knox to see what is known as "ruby silver." There was not a great deal of this type of quartz in Tonopah, but in the Montana it showed up in pockets. This first time I saw it, the twenty-foot stope looked as if the walls had been spattered with blood. When I held a piece of it up to the light, it glowed like a jewel — very exotic stuff. However, the color faded quickly when exposed to the air. Every time a face of ruby silver appeared in a mine, people clamored to see it.

I went underground many times in the years I spent in Tonopah, often hanging on to the skip, which is no more than a cross-piece hung to a single rope. Sometimes I rode the rim of the bucket, or was safely deposited inside the bucket, which, after all, was a little more comfortable for a tenderfoot.

An entertainment of uncommon interest that first year was a dramatic reading of Julius Caesar by Herman W. Knickerbocker. This gentleman had come to Hugh's office some days before to ask him if he had any of Shakespeare's plays. When he saw my husband's full set of Shakespeare, he asked if he could borrow *Julius Caesar,* without telling Hugh anything of his plans.

My husband knew Mr. Knickerbocker by reputation, and like many men who are too self-contained to be flashy, Hugh had a secret admiration for any man who was definitely spectacular. He relished telling me the tales that were floating through camp about this gentleman. One whispered story told of Mr. Knickerbocker's having been ruined by an illicit love; another maintained he had assumed a debt incurred by some absconding relative. He had been a minister, that was sure; that he was from the South was evident in his speech. But whether he had actually been the pastor of a fashionable New Orleans church and tried for heresy and unfrocked was something else again. Anyway, no man so handsome could escape curious comment.

This reading was held in the Opera House, a large barn of a place with a stage at one end and a shallow balcony at the other. The admission was a dollar a seat, and I think the "star" made enough to insure a grubstake for many days.

Mr. Knickerbocker, in dress suit, walked onto the dimly lighted stage. He was tall and slender, with straight features and black hair. By way of introduction he said: "You may wonder at my temerity in presenting to you such a performance in this environment, but a prospector named Knickerbocker, down on his luck, needs a grubstake. And a man must use the tools he understands."

He read the play brilliantly in a rich, clear, expressive voice. I felt he had missed his calling as an actor, as ministers so often do.

Not only the reading made that evening exciting. In the middle of the tender scene between Brutus and his wife, a dogfight started in the balcony. Suddenly there was a terrific growling and scrambling, with people fleeing in all directions from a howling mass of dogs, which were finally kicked down the rickety stairs and out the door. Where upon, Mr. Knickerbocker made some remark to the effect that now that the other dogs had a chance to perform, this dog would continue.

Entertainments on the frontier always ended with a dance, and this evening was no exception. The chairs were pushed back against the wall, but just as the banjo and piano players entered, two shots were fired outside the building. The curious crowd rushed toward the entrance, flinging open the doors. Two more shots followed in rapid succession and landed somewhere inside the hall. As the shots continued to come into the hall, everyone surged back toward the center of the room and began scrambling for shelter.

Grabbing me by the hand, Hugh said in his deliberate way, "Marjorie, I don't know what to do with you," and then noticing the piano, shoved me behind it. I had no intention of missing anything, so, as Hugh turned away, I poked my head up over the piano. But, to my disappointment, nothing more happened. No one was hurt, and no one questioned the right of a husband to take a few shots at the man who threatened the sanctity of his home. While the affair concerned figures about town well known to us all, it can best be summed up in the words of the newsboy calling the next day: "All about the bum shootin' by the crazy loon."

Most of Hugh's friends were members of the Mizpah Club, a group of old-timers, men who had been in Tonopah since the establishment of the camp or at least had arrived before 1903. I think Hugh was the founder; at least he was the secretary for the first year. In the clubroom over the post office, the members played cards endlessly, talking the regular mining-camp jargon: new discoveries, location work, claims jumped, etc.

Fifty members of this club had presented us with a full set of flat silver as a wedding present, and the first task I set for myself was the writing of fifty notes of thanks to these gentlemen. Knowing the notes would certainly be compared, I was careful to make the wording of each note different, a task that kept me occupied for quite a while.

No women were allowed in the clubroom, but once a year on the Fourth of July, they slicked up their quarters and invited the ladies to be their guests. Just as I expected, at the reception that first year, the notes of acknowledgement came under discussion. One of the men, Dick Dunlap, called my attention to the fact that I had signed my name "Marjorie Moore" and then had attempted to erase "Moore" and substitute my new name, "Brown," with indifferent success.

"But," he added playfully, "when I see you look at Hugh, I can see

Marjorie Moore has really been erased by Marjorie Brown."

I don't know whether my husband actually accepted that idea. He used to say I was the brimstone end of the match and he was the stick. He and Dick Dunlap spent a good deal of time teasing me. Hugh delighted in quips like this, "Dick asked me if the climate agreed with my wife. I told him that was more than I could ask of any climate." And, what is more, Hugh always said I asked his advice only so that I could be sure of making up my mind in the opposite direction.

The Mizpah clubroom didn't boast much in the way of furniture, a few ordinary office tables and an old Morris chair (they were everywhere in the camp). But the pictures on the walls were of great interest; Tonopah's first tent, the first frame building, the first shaft, and so on. One that impressed me for its comic pathos was a tree constructed of thin strips of wood ripped from packing boxes and nailed to the sides of a two-by-four. On the end of each limb was suspended an Edam cheese, big and red and round. Under the photograph was inscribed:

THE NEVERGREEN TREE
Tonopah's first Christmas tree
1901

One could not help laughing at it, but it made me sad, too. The tree was such a wistful testimony to holiday loneliness.

As the population of the camp increased, Christmas festivities became more lavish. My first contribution to these gala evenings came in 1904, when one of the club members invited me to sing a solo. I was delighted to accept, but there was no piano in the clubroom to accompany me. Will Towne played the guitar, and we had performed together many times; but he said he couldn't get off the night shift until eleven o'clock, and by the time he went home and changed his clothes, the party would be over. The club representative told him to come ahead in his work clothes. It would take fifteen minutes to get down off the hill, so we would look for him at eleven-fifteen. Will Towne, field engineer and geologist by affinity, played the guitar with a flair. There were few pianos in town, at least uptown, so Will carried his instrument with him wherever he went in the evening. His work clothes added the element of contrast so constantly present in our lives, for I was all decked out in fluffy white organdy, with my hair parted in the middle and coiled softly at the back of my head, and a deep red silk rose tucked behind my ear. Will Towne was handsome in brown khaki and wool shirt, with one high-shod leg resting on a chair, guitar on his knee, his fingers skimming the strings as he followed my thin young voice with his improvised accompaniment. We sang "Mandalay," but not to the familiar brisk marching tune. In the early nineteen-hundreds there was an original melody, plaintive and nostalgic, and I sang verses that are forgotten now. It was a successful occasion for both of us and led to many repetitions in the years to come.

*Cowhand's Luck ... Goldfield ..."Richest Ore Ever
Recorded"... Lady in a Flophouse ... Great Mines of
Goldfield ... Of Games and Gamblers ... Gun Play
for Elinor Glyn ... The Gans-Nelson Fight ...
High-Graders, Mine Owners, and the I.W.W.*

BY ALL ODDS the most captivating mining tale that ever came out of
Nevada is the story of Nixon and Wingfield, which is the beginning of
the story of Goldfield. This is the way it was told to me.

It all began in 1902, when George Nixon was a middle-aged bank
clerk in a little cattle town in northern Nevada called Winnemucca.
One day a young man in blue jeans and a broad Stetson stepped up to
his window holding in his hand a solitaire diamond ring.

"How much will you lend me on this stone?" asked the man.

Nixon looked at it. "Well," he answered, "it looks like a nice stone,
but I'll have to have it appraised before I can tell you what the bank
will lend on it."

"Listen, mister," the stranger broke in, "I'm not asking the bank,
I'm asking you. I want you to lend me the money on face value. How
about $250?"

"Who are you and where did you come from?" asked the banker.

"George Wingfield, and I come from Oregon. I been punching cows
here in Winnemucca. There's a strike down at Tonopah. The place is
booming, and I want to get in on it. You and I will go fifty-fifty on
everything."

Mr. Nixon took time to give the young man a long penetrating
scrutiny. Then he turned away. When he came back, he handed Wingfield $250. At that moment was formed the partnership that sent the
bank clerk to the United States Senate and made the cowhand the
richest man in Nevada.

George Wingfield came to Tonopah and opened a gambling house
called the Tonopah Club, and his patrons believed in, and depended
upon, his fair play as they counted on tomorrow's sun. Whether George
Nixon's money was used to buy the card tables, the roulette wheel, and
the crap layout, I don't know; but when Wingfield asked for the loan,
he said "fifty-fifty on everything." So if the money began spiraling with
the opening of the Tonopah Club, it is but one more illustration of the
making of United States senators in the West.

By the time George Wingfield arrived in Tonopah, the ground nearby had been staked out for miles, but in the Tonopah Club he came in

contact with men itching for a grubstake. He selected a smart half-breed Indian named Harry Stimler, who started into the desert searching for silver. At a spot about thirty miles south of Tonopah called Rabbit Springs, Stimler picked up a piece of interesting float. But it was not silver that he held in his hand; it was gold! A terrific sandstorm was blowing that day, but in spite of the misery and cold, Stimler traced the ledge from which the float had rolled and staked out several claims, one of which he called the "Sandstorm" in honor of the weather. This was December 2, 1902.

Through 1903 the activity around Goldfield, touched off by the rich samples brought into Tonopah by Harry Stimler, moved forward without the richness of the district being really proven; but by spring of 1904 the location work established the fabulous surface values, and the shaft began to prove there was richness with depth. The boom reached the boiling point.

George Wingfield bought the Sandstorm from Harry Stimler, and it produced seven million dollars in seven months. This is only one of the incredible items connected with Rabbit Springs, which later became Goldfield, the richest gold discovery ever made anywhere in the world. In order to escape expensive litigation, George Wingfield bought and combined many contiguous claims and fractions into one group he called the "Goldfield Consolidated Mines Company" and capitalized the company for fifty million shares, most of which were traded on the Mining Exchange in San Francisco.

The richest single shipment from Goldfield was forty-seven and one-half tons from the Hays-Monette lease on the Mohawk Mine. It was so rich that the ore was sacked and stored in the John S. Cooke Bank until it could be shipped. When it reached the Selby Smelters near Oakland, California, it was tested and valued at $574,953.39. The record shows this as the richest shipment of ore ever recorded in the world, both in value per ton ($12,300) and in over-all value.

Goldfield was the scene of the wildest mining boom Nevada had experienced since Comstock days. Stages loaded with prospectors, promoters, gamblers, and ladies of doubtful design were coming into Tonopah, two and three a day, stopping only long enough for a change of horses before pushing on to the newest El Dorado. Many of our friends bought claims from the army of prospectors who had staked out the desert for miles around the original spots located by Harry Stimler, by Al Meyers and Charlie Taylor, two other lucky first arrivals.

As a result of the earlier Tonopah excitement, prospectors had swarmed over southern Nevada like field mice. Hardly more than wanderers, most of them knew nothing of mineral formation, but now groups of men in eastern cities stood ready to grubstake any man on the scene willing to undertake the search for gold. Other men were hired to follow the trails of the prospectors to report any discoveries that looked promising.

Hugh acquired no claims in Goldfield, but the "get-rich-quick" fever is easy to catch from others. The first time I felt this burning sensation was the night two of our friends came hotfoot up the hill in great excitement to show us a panning they had brought in that afternoon from their Goldfield lease. In the bottom of a little frying pan was a teaspoonful of sand so yellow it shrieked "wealth" even to my uninitiated eyes. Gold found on your own ground!

My first trip to Goldfield was in August 1904. Hugh had business there, and of course I was crazy to see the excitement at first hand. But the sleeping accommodations were so meager that Hugh hesitated to have me make the trip. When Hugh's client, Lucian L. Patrick, a promoter, told him we could "bunk" with him and his wife, we accepted the welcome invitation. The Patricks were building a house and living in it while the carpenters worked around them. If we were game enough to sleep on a mattress on the floor, they would be glad to have us.

We hired a buckboard and team, and started out just after the day's heat had died down. The desert is always cool at night, so we knew we would have a comfortable trip; but although Goldfield was only about thirty miles away, we took a wrong fork in the road, and were delayed for more than a hour.

We stopped for dinner at Klondike Wells, from which Jim Butler had been traveling when he made the silver strike at Tonopah. That meal at Klondike was typical of many I recall on the desert — sliced tomatoes curled at the edges by the hot dry air, greasy stew or boiled beef, lifeless watery mashed potatoes, and canned corn, with the inevitable baking powder biscuits, cold and crumbly and tasteless. I remember the kitchen and the cook, too, with his dirty apron and blue shirt, his shaggy mustache stained with tobacco. I have thought many times how lucky it was that I was too young to be fastidious, and hungry enough to be blind. It was food, and I ate. After dinner we continued our trip into the night.

As it turned out, we slept in the very kind of shelter Hugh had tried to avoid. We arrived in Goldfield so much later than we had expected that Hugh decided to seek some place to sleep and arrive at the Patricks' in the morning. But the only type of sleeping quarters available was technically known as a "flop house," a big tent divided by canvas partitions into cubicles about ten feet square. We were ushered quietly into one of these "roomettes," where I could just distinguish a three-quarter size iron bed, a wash bowl and pitcher, and one chair. A sickly light from a small electric bulb somewhere in the distance served for illumination, and a chorus of snores told us we were not alone. I didn't attempt to examine the bedding. I wouldn't have been able to see it, anyway, in that dim light, but I wasn't as squeamish as I had been a year earlier as a bride. All I really cared about was to dust off my hair with a towel from my handbag, clean my face with cold cream and fall into bed.

Presently I felt something bulging heavily against me, and it wasn't my husband. It was our unknown neighbor on the other side of the canvas partition. I wriggled away. In such restricted quarters, it was no use. That unwanted bulge stayed with me most of the night. I have often wondered if we ever met.

The next morning we arrived at the Patricks'. They had been mildly concerned about us when we didn't show up the night before, but desert travel was so uncertain that no one worried very much about people being overdue. Their house was hardly more than a shell, and we did sleep on the floor. Since there were no windows in yet, we dressed and undressed in a closet. We ate from a table consisting of planks set across two sawhorses and had a wonderful time.

Of course, it was the mines that absorbed our attention. They really were not mines, hardly more than shallow holes, but already fortunes had been scooped off the surface, loaded into canvas bags, and started off to the smelters in California or Colorado. We visited all the famous leases: the Hays-Monette, the Sandstorm, the Jumbo, the January, the White Horse, the Red Top — names indicative of something lucky to the men who had staked them out. We saw Mr. Vermilliar, a lawyer from Tonopah, standing guard with a shotgun in a little excavation no bigger than a bathroom, where, with his own hands, he had scooped out $100,000. For weeks, day and night, he stayed there guarding his unprotected mint with an armchair down in the hole where he could catch forty winks when he thought it was safe. We walked over the spot where fabulously rich ore had been uncovered when the two owners dug grooves for the ore car rails. We also saw the claim that became the Mohawk Mine and made millionaires of George Wingfield and George Nixon.

In spite of desert sun and dusty streets, Tonopah loved a parade. Here a troupe of entertainers drum up business. Sign in foreground offers: "A Nice New Bed 7.50 a Month or 50¢ a Night."

The grandest celebration of them all: Railroad Days, 1904, when the shortline from Tonopah Junction finally linked us with civilization. Jim Butler's history-making burro "marched" in the parade.

For weeks committees worked on plans for literary exercises, contests, street dances, fireworks—all to celebrate the arrival of the railroad. But for the children, the highlight was J. H. Hall's free ice cream and lemonade.

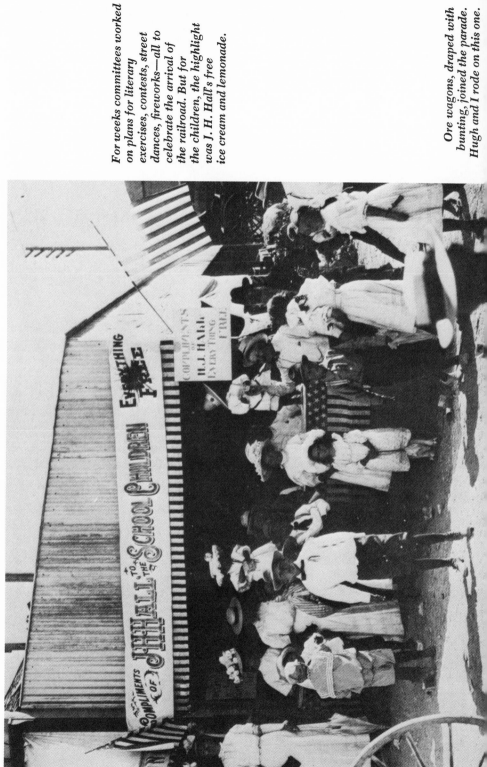

Ore wagons, draped with bunting, joined the parade. Hugh and I rode on this one.

Late in the afternoon there was a tug-o'-war between
men from the West End and the Extension.
When their faces started to turn black,
I didn't stay to watch!

The double-handed drilling contest—a unique event of mining-town celebrations. One partner holds the drill; the other swings a sixteen-pound hammer. When the blow connects, the drill bites deep into a huge block of granite (under the platform). But if it misses by even a fraction of an inch, a man's hand may be crushed.

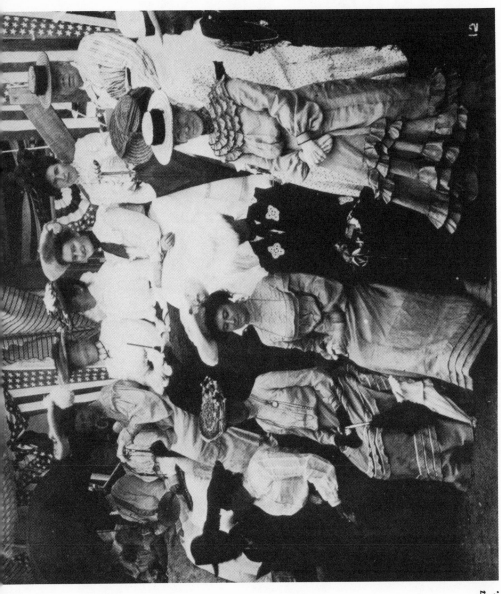

Waiting for the Railroad Days parade. We had "box" seats in Hugh's office window (center of picture).

The ladies in the bleachers: a gallery of boomtown types.

*More bunting—this for the Fourth of July, 1905. Tall man in
center is Zeb Kendall, prospector, promoter, and gambler.
After making and losing several fortunes, he moved on to
Virginia City, where he made still another from tailings left
by miners back in the '70s.*

During the evening, we drifted through the streets of Goldfield. Every other building was a saloon and gambling house, all crowded with men in high boots and wide felt hats, with six-shooters often in open evidence, and here and there a bright bit of color testifying to a feminine clientele.

Along the way we heard chatter about this man or that gambling for high stakes in this saloon or another. Our acquaintance from Tonopah, Herman Knickerbocker, had come to Goldfield when it began to boom. He became an intense and silent gambler, playing for absurdly high stakes, winning and losing fortunes in a night. And he dressed the part: grey Stetson, long black Prince Albert coat, dark trousers stuffed into high boots, white shirt, and black string tie, the flowing ends of which waved over his shoulder just like the gamblers in a western movie. He wore his hair a bit long, even for that day, and carried himself like an adventurer, with a wide and swinging gait, a voice musical and low, and an over-all aloof melancholy that seemed to preclude his ever being called by his first name. Mr. Knickerbocker was without exception the handsomest and most authentic westerner I ever saw, perhaps because of the streak of drama in his nature.

One incident convinced me that I was not a born gambler. As we passed Tex Richard's "Northern," I poked my head through an open window level with the street. The roulette wheel was directly inside, the dealer standing in shirt sleeves and vest. From my vantage point I could see the faces of the men at the table, many unshaven, others as well groomed as any man anywhere. Mr. Patrick threw a twenty-dollar gold piece onto his favorite number. Someone tossed a ten-dollar gold piece. It landed on the black, and was allowed to stay there. Others followed suit. A turn of the little wheel, and a good-sized sum of money was swept out of the hands of my friends, people who had just stopped at a window to get a glimpse of what was going on inside. No one seemed to think anything of the fact that all that money had been wiped out on one turn of a little wheel, just to give a girl a thrill. Hugh and I both played the stock market and won and lost heavily. But I never lost my secret fear of gaming tables induced by that walk downtown one night in Goldfield in 1904.

Judge Kenneth Jackson, a fellow-traveler on our first trip to Tonopah, was with us that night. As he walked beside me, shielding me from the crowd with quiet southern courtesy, he talked about our future, Hugh's and mine. He always treated us with a fatherly benevolence.

Hugh and I had a great opportunity in Nevada, he thought. We should set ourselves to make a hundred thousand dollars and clear out. That was enough to make anyone comfortable but not enough to be a burden.

"A hundred thousand?" I said. "We'll make three times that amount before we leave. Why not?" He looked at me indulgently.

"Well," he said, "when you set your sights too high, you're likely to miss your objective."

But I laughed at his admonition. At that moment Goldfield was at the height of its boom, and Tonopah had settled down to steady production of a million dollars a month. Anything was possible. Why not for us?

After our tour of the town we sat over a cold drink in the Patricks' dining room, and "L.L.," as Hugh called him, told us how he had secured the claims that became part of the Mohawk. Mr. Patrick had been commissioned by a group of Chicago capitalists to look over the Tonopah discovery. He had come too late for the Tonopah strike, but his arrival was exactly timed to acquire ground in Goldfield. He talked Charlie Taylor into a $75,000 option on three claims. Five thousand dollars was to be paid in ten days, the rest in three months.

The district looked so promising that the claims Mr. Patrick had optioned were considered to be worth three times $75,000. There were men with ready cash, clamoring to pay Charlie Taylor any amount if he would break his contract with Lucian Patrick. But the two cardinal sins on the frontier are to break one's word and to be disloyal to a friend. Prospectors seldom welch. Charlie Taylor stood pat.

The day when the option was to be taken up, for some reason the money had not reached the bank. There were no banking facilities or telegraph in Goldfield, so all the principals were in Tonopah. The money was to be telegraphed to the Nye County Bank.

"L.L. was in my office all that day," Hugh explained. "I thought he was going to wear a hole in my floor and drop right through into the bank saloon. He thrashed up and down that room, back and forth, back and forth. We had arranged with George Richard to signal the moment the money came if it did arrive before the bank closed."

"I was so nervous, I sweated like a horse," said Lucian. "I couldn't understand why in hell the money didn't come. They had telegraphed me earlier that week that everything was okay. But there it was two o'clock and no money, and two men ready to grab my option at three, when the bank would close. Down the street were knots of men, buttonholing Charlie Taylor, talking, speculating on what had happened, some of them even betting on whether the money would show up in time. At ten minutes to three Hugh saw George come out of the bank waving a piece of paper.

"God! I just couldn't look," continued Lucian. "I was so worn out I just sat down . . ."

The news spread like sparks sputtering from a fuse. Men everywhere came running together. Hugh had to drag Lucian to his feet and almost carry him over to the bank. And the money was paid out in gold.

"In gold?" I exclaimed. "Five thousand dollars in gold?"

"Five thousand dollars," returned Lucian Patrick. And then all the men came whirling around him.

"We should have put you down the Desert Queen shaft and kept you there until after banking hours!" they were yelling at him. "It was highway robbery for those claims to go for $75,000!"

Most of the dashing young men in Tonopah moved to Goldfield. Tonopah holdings had quickly been consolidated into big companies, while in Goldfield a young man could compete with other gay blades who were bent on making fortunes but determined to have a "helluva good time" on the way. Because we lived in Tonopah, I was not too familiar with the racy happenings in Goldfield, where life was always more spectacular than ours. Echoes of excitement filtered into our town — for instance, the "Wild West" stunt staged for Elinor Glyn, author of *Three Weeks,* the most sensational novel of the 1900's.

In 1905, with hoopla and fanfare, Elinor Glyn was brought from Los Angeles to "see the sights" of the new boomtown. In order to make the gambling look colossal, all the money in town was gathered onto the gaming tables in Tex Rickard's Northern, including cash from the John S. Cooke Bank. John S. Cooke was something of a sport and a tremendous Goldfield booster. The money was said to have been strictly tabulated and returned next day to its legitimate owners.

At a given signal, trouble was started at one of the roulette tables. There was real gun play; heroes sprang to the rescue. Elinor Glyn wanted local color, and she got it. The event — in actuality a colossal advertising stunt — secured headlines in newspapers throughout the country, which was the reason for it in the first place.

In 1906 Goldfield boosters arranged the Gans-Nelson fight, also for publicity purposes. By that time, the railroad had been completed from Tonopah into Goldfield, and special trains ran from San Francisco and from as far east as Chicago, bringing thousands from all over the United States. The winner of this thirty-round battle for the lightweight championship of the world was to receive $30,000, and this amount in twenty-dollar gold pieces was on display in the window of the John S. Cooke Bank. Gans won the bout on a foul, and received one thousand dollars per round. As a result of this event, plenty of money found its way into mining stock promotion, and much "sucker" money was left behind in the gambling houses run by Ole Elliott, Tex Rickard, and the rest of the fraternity of saloon-keepers.

Goldfield became the scene of serious labor troubles, which developed out of the flagrant practice of high-grading, that is, the theft by mine employees of lumps of exceptionally high-grade ore. High-grading was so openly practiced that the miners scarcely tried to conceal it. A man was pointed out to me on the street whose clothes were so heavily loaded with rocks that he swayed when he walked. In spite of this lack of concealment, it was not easy to arrest a man for high-grading. He had to be caught with the ore on his person, and the ore had to be identified as having come from a specific spot, a difficult procedure since all ore in the district was similar. Usually when a high-grader came off a shift, he had a confederate at hand to whisk the loot into the hands of a local assayer, who quickly reduced the rocks to powder so that the ore could not be identified. Sometimes the ore was shipped to Tonopah. Once it was out of town, the high-grader was pretty sure to be safe.

When mine owners tried to curb the looting of rich ore pockets, labor organizers in the International Workers of the World swarmed into Goldfield, and a few men were killed. Captain Case, a companion of our stagecoach honeymoon, figured, and not too well, in these negotiations. In dealing with the miners, he was arrogant and unyielding, as might have been expected from his university and military background.

The mine operators employed men to buddy around with suspected high-graders, trap them into drinking, and capture them with the rocks still in their possession. It was a dangerous and exciting game, and once I had a glimpse of the danger.

One night about midnight we were awakened by someone scuffing clumsily up the steps. Hugh answered the loud knocking to find at the door a young man, roughly dressed and spattered with blood. He told excitedly of having captured two men who had been suspected of high-grading. He had locked them in a room behind the Sagebrush Club. Hugh was needed to complete the formalities of their arrest. There had been a rainstorm earlier in the evening, and the flashes of lightning and murmurs of thunder rolling away into the mountains emphasized my feeling of possible danger to my husband. I pleaded with him not to go.

Hugh said quietly, "You wouldn't have me shirk my duty because it was dangerous, would you? Nothing will happen to me." Nothing did happen to Hugh, of course, but stolen wealth and danger in the night were pretty heady stuff. I was never allowed to forget I was living in Boomtown.

Governor Sparks was at last prevailed upon by the Mine Operators' Association to appeal to President Theodore Roosevelt to send troops into Goldfield "to keep the peace." At that time there was no state militia or police force in Nevada. It was a real shock to see soldiers marching through our streets, when they arrived in Tonopah on their way to Goldfield. Much criticism was leveled at Governor Sparks as well as the mine operators for making the appeal, but the incident pointed up the fact that a state law enforcement department was needed in Nevada.

*Short Line from Tonopah Junction . . ."Railroad Days"
. . . Indians, Floats, and the Carson Band . . . Prize
Money for the Losers . . . The Governor's
Gunman and Others . . . A Drilling Contest*

RAILROAD DAYS — July 25, 26, and 27, 1904. Days are milestones in life, and certainly these days were milestones in Tonopah's life and mine.

July 25 had been selected as the date for the driving of the last spike — a gold one, of course — to mark the completion of the railroad between Tonopah Junction, a few miles south of Sodaville, and Tonopah. Sodaville, you will remember, was the place where, on our wedding journey, we changed for "all points in the world," as the conductor told us. Now the track had been extended east to Tonopah, and the days of the stagecoach and twenty-mule team were drawing to an end.

A three-day celebration was planned. For weeks committees had been working on details: literary exercises, music, decorations, games, drilling, free lemonade and ice cream, dancing, fireworks. The whole world was invited. Also coming to town was the "Carson Band," a group of young businessmen from Carson City who played at every notable event in Nevada.

For several months Hugh and I had sauntered each evening to the brow of the hill, whence we could view the sunset and at the same time watch the daily progress of the distant speck on the desert that we knew was the railroad construction camp. To my ever-dramatic mind, the camp, as it grew larger with its slow advance, had all the elements of a deliverer.

By the middle of July it was a fifty-fifty gamble as to whether the rails would actually be in place in time for the celebration to proceed on schedule. Every available man was hired, and many men in town volunteered their services. As a result, the road was graded, the ties placed, and the rails laid. The engine was run over the rails and spikes were driven into the rails behind the engine. Anything and everything was done that would help to lay the last few miles of track before the appointed day.

About five o'clock in the afternoon of July 24, the last rail was in place, the engine pulled into the freight yard, and every mine whistle in the district turned loose to let us know the celebration was really on. But no one knew even then whether the track could be made safe for the special trains to roll over them into the Tonopah station, trains that were already on their way from Reno, Carson City, and even from California. On the edge of town, huge bonfires made great pools of light, in which we could see men and horses sweating and straining to anchor the rails to the ties. In case the track could not be used, Tasker Oddie's teams would stand by to haul the passengers that last quarter mile.

Sometime around daybreak I awoke suddenly to a sound on the air — music! band music! from somewhere far off. Cold shivers ran through me, and I wept softly, much to Hugh's puzzlement. Never have I heard music more tremblingly beautiful than the distant strains of the Carson Band on its way uptown from the station in that early morning of July 25, 1904.

The day dawned clear and hot. At eight o'clock the celebration started with the detonation of several rounds of powder from the top of Mount Oddie. As early as possible I dragged Hugh downtown, determined not to miss a thing. Many of the events took place on the two main streets, now hung with flags and festooned with colorful bunting. Knowing that we would have a ringside seat, we had invited our little coterie of friends to come to Hugh's office in the Golden Block and enjoy the sights from the cool vantage point of its wide windows.

The day was a welding of the pageantry of the Old West and the New: Indians, cowboys, ranchers, miners, prospectors, soldiers of fortune. Each group had its sprinkling of women and children, all decked out for the holiday; and there was something for everybody.

At ten o'clock came the parade with handsome old John Cuddy at its head, mounted on a brown horse, his white hair and flowing mustache making him every inch the Marshall of the Parade. Behind him, in blue and white uniform, marched the Carson Band, followed by Indians in full regalia, eagle-feather headdress, fringed deerskin, and all. In the center of the parade came one of Tasker's road-grading wagons turned into a float, on which rode four young girls with fluttering white dresses and flowing hair. After them came a tent mounted on a small truck pulled by a couple of young men. Tied to the back of the truck was a little grey burro, and fastened to his harness was a canvas banner that read, ME AND JIM FOUND TONOPAH. A troop of yelling cowboys and stragglers brought up the rear.

One of the young ladies from the float, Miss Belle Pepper, was crowned Queen of Railroad Days in a pretty ceremony on the platform erected in the center of the street. This was followed by "literary exer-

71

cises" consisting of a stirring speech and closing with a solo by Lenore Sollender. Then we all trooped down to the railroad yard to see the driving of the golden spike.

The afternoon, although very hot, was given over to races and contests: pie-eating, where little boys emerged from a tussle with blackberry pie looking as if they had been attacked by swarming bees; ladies' nail-driving contests, where women of all ages drove nails into a plank, hitting more fingernails than wire ones; races of every description for all ages, sexes, and nationalities.

At the scene of the contests and races, Al Meyers was king. Al, one of the original locators of Goldfield, along with Charlie Taylor and Harry Stimler, had made a fabulous fortune through the sale of his claims. On this day he became a self-constituted dispenser of prize money, standing in the center of the street and singling out disconsolate losers. "Hey, you there! Tell the kid with the freckles to come here." Over and over again I heard him call to some youngster in the crowd. "Did you get a prize?"

"No, sir."

"Why sure you did. Here, here's a dollar. That's third prize. You ran a fine race. Here, you go over there and tell that fellow you want some ice cream. Is this your sister? No? Well, you take her along anyway. Hey, what's the matter, a big galoot like you comin' in fourth? Here! Now go get yourself an ice cream soda. Go on. Quit cryin'!"

"Aw, I ain't cryin'!"

"Sure you are. They can hear ya bawlin' way over to Goldfield. Go drown yer sorrow in a soda mug. Go on."

"Gee, thanks, mister. Hey, fellas! He gave me five dollars! Come on!"

"What's the matter, lady? Ya didn't miss them nails, by any chance? Yea, sure, that's strawberry jam on your fingers. Well, here, go buy the old man a drink. Tell 'im you got first prize for bein' game. Tell 'im I said so."

All afternoon, out in the hot sun, Al Myers picked losers and handed out dollars. Many men have that sympathetic impulse to comfort the loser, but few have the chance or the wherewithal to accomplish it.

Later that night we heard that Al was down in a back room of the Merchants Hotel playing roulette with twenty-dollar gold pieces, five to each turn of the wheel. It was always a show when any of the big gamblers got to playing for high stakes, so we went down to swell the crowd standing in the shadows watching. Al Meyers on one side of the table under the big light and the dealer on the other, the little ball spinning, dropping at last into a slot with that unmistakable click that breaks the breathless tension.

What Al Meyers lost that night was up in the thousands. His money didn't last very long, but while it did, he lived his idea of a king's life. That's something of which few of us can boast.

Many spectacular figures were in evidence during the celebration. Hugh called my attention to Governor John Sparks, walking down the street with another man. The man with the governor, Hugh told me, was Jack Davis, Sparks' hired gunman. January Jones and his pal Bar Francis swaggered down the street among the merrymakers, too, both ostentatiously carrying their guns.

During the celebration I also had a glimpse of Harry Ramsey, which explained to me somewhat his reputation as a cold, deliberate killer. I wanted to feel the excitement of the contests at close range, so I left the vantage point of Hugh's office window to skirt the crowd below. Looking through the mass of spectators, I caught sight of Harry Ramsey as he faced a man in front of him, his lips taut and his eyes glistening. In a moment the other man scuttled away. I would like to have known what Harry Ramsey's next move would have been if his antagonist had not disappeared, for every time I recall the incident, it gives me the same shiver I had that day.

The second Railroad Day was marked by a unique event of mining-town celebrations, the double-handed drilling contest. Two men work as a team, with steel drills and a hammer weighing sixteen pounds, to drill holes in granite, competing with other teams for prizes running into hundreds of dollars. A drilling contest is the most exciting exhibition of skill and courage I know of. Today it is a thing of the past. When machine drills were invented, hand drilling was over; but in 1904, miners drilled in competition to prove who had the surest aim, the quickest stroke, and the strongest arm. Under the platform in the center of the street was a huge block of granite, a selected piece of Gunnison granite hauled in by mule team from Colorado for the occasion. The top of the block was flush with the floor of the platform, and into this rock each two-man team would drill for fifteen minutes. The pair reaching the greatest depth was the winner.

The team, with its seconds, comes onto the platform, stripped to the waist. One man carries the hammers, and his partner carries a long, heavy roll of canvas, which contains the two sets of drills, sharpened for the contest. Each drill is about an inch in diameter, and they vary in length from a foot to four feet.

Each man has his own hammer and set of drills. All are carefully laid out in precise order after being examined by an impartial official. The short drills are placed near at hand, the longer ones at the back within reach. Then, with infinite care, each team selects the spot in the granite boulder where they will drill. Granite has seams that are often harder or softer than the rest of the rock, so the spot selected is important.

Two men get into position, one crouching down and clasping the shortest drill close around the head, his partner standing over him, his hammer uplifted, ready to deliver the first blow. The timer gives the signal by touching him on the shoulder.

The first tap of the hammer is soft, just enough to give the drill a straight push, for the hole must be started straight. The next blow is a bit harder, and by the fourth blow, or the fifth, the hole is on its way, and the man's body bends to the blows as they grow more and more powerful.

A slow-running hose attached to a barrel pours water into the hole as the man crouching over the drill moves it skillfully up and down and around after each hammer blow. At all costs the steel must be kept from sticking in the rock. If a drill sticks —"fitchered," they call it — precious seconds are lost, for it must be tapped loose before it can be struck again. If it does not spring loose, the spectators know it will break off, and the unlucky pair must start a new hole.

Every thirty seconds the partners change places. When the moment approaches for the change, the man holding the drill grasps his own hammer with one hand and gives the drill one last turn with the other, while the timer, watch in hand, touches the standing partner on the shoulder. At the signal the man flings his hammer aside, then crouches down and grabs the drill with both hands as his partner springs to his feet ready to deliver the next blow. The new man on the hammer comes down without missing the rhythm of a stroke or the fraction of a second.

As the depth of the hole increases and a longer steel is necessary, the first drill must be jerked out and the new one inserted without breaking the rhythm of the hammer. This is easy when the drills are short, but when a three-foot steel must be yanked out and a four-foot one dropped unerringly into the inch-wide hole, the maneuver must be accomplished with unerring precision. If the drill is lifted a fraction of a second too slowly, a stroke can be lost, which can mean a half inch at the finish.

Listen to the crowd! Cheers, catcalls. Bets are yelled out. "Lean on that stick there!" "Two to one on this team!" "We got our money on ya, Bill!" "I'll take ya!" "Put 'er down, boys!" Twelve minutes. Thirteen, fourteen! The timer lifts his hand above the bending backs. The hammer blows quicken. The crowd sways and murmurs. Fifteen minutes! The hand descends.

The drillers stand panting while every drop of water is sucked out of the hole, and the officials insert the measuring rod. The crowd is still. The official straightens up and bellows: "Thirty-nine and one-half inches!" More cheers, a few groans, more betting. By this time, the next team is in place, and their followers are cheering for them.

A drilling contest has everything: technique, beauty, endurance, speed, and danger. If the hammer descends a fraction of an inch out of line on the tiny head of the drill, a man's hand may be crushed.

Once during my life in Tonopah I saw a man's hand struck. Suddenly the hammer poised in midair. The crowd groaned, knowing what had happened. After an instant flinch, the man crouched over the drill, looked up at his towering partner, and yelled, "Come down, you!" Down came the hammer. The men cheered and the women cried. The hand on the drill began to turn red, but still it held on to the drill. When the injured man's turn came to rise and hold the hammer, the blood crept down his arm until it looked as if it had been thrust into a pot of red paint. The blood ran into the hole and mixed with water from the hose. Everytime the hammer descended, the red fluid sloshed up and spattered nearby onlookers. The man sagged lower after every blow, but he never gave up until the timer's hand signaled fifteen minutes. Then he fell over in a dead faint. The platform looked like a slaughtering block.

Champion drillers were kings, known and feted throughout the mining world. The prize money was accompanied by cases of champagne and other liquors.

The third day's celebration consisted of a single-handed drilling contest, cowboy races, bucking contests, and a baseball game. Late in the afternoon we went down near the railroad to see the tug-of-war, but when the men turned black, it made me sick and I fled. Every night there was dancing, and on the last evening, a display of fire-works.

At regular intervals during the three days' celebration, mule-drawn trucks, loaded with high-grade ore from leases in Goldfield, creaked through town. One shipment had canvas streamers running along the sides of the wagon, which announced in letters three feet high: "30 TONS OF ORE! $45,000."

A photograph taken that day shows Hugh and me standing on the ore sacks along with the lucky owners and several of our friends. Astride the wheel horse was long, lean Harry Hudson, a master mule-skinner who could turn a twenty-mule team on a twenty-foot square. That day his slender body assumed more than the usual stiffness of pride as he rode through the town, for in front of him perched his eighteen-month-old baby. A canvas runner floating in front of them bore the inscription: HARRY HUDSON AND SON.

A New House ... Mission Furniture and Inside
Plumbing! ... An Elegant Social with Music from
the Redlight ... Of Baby Food and Frontier
Doctors ... The Wonderful Vacuum Cleaner ...
Fire! ... Some Unforgettable Household Helpers

IN THE FALL OF 1905, our stay in Tonopah was beginning to take on an
air of permanence. In addition, we were excitedly anticipating the birth
of our first child, and so we began to think seriously of a home of our
own. I wanted to build where we used to walk out at sunset to watch
the progress of the railroad construction camp. From there our windows would face a hundred miles of uninterrupted grandeur with, at
nightfall, the pageantry of sunsets that only desert air and far horizons
can produce. In the middle distance lay a clump of low hills, so washed
by centuries of rain that mineral deposits had come to the surface in
patches of color: red, purple and deep yellow, looking like pigments on
an artist's palette. But my husband thought the view would not com-
pensate for the winter winds, and of course he was right, though I re-
gretted the loss of all that beauty beyond our windows.

I had been getting progressively more homesick for San Francisco as
the months wore on. Now that the railroad was here, I could make the
trip in ease, and I had a real reason for going — furnishings for our
new home! So I boarded the train with happy anticipation.

As the ferryboat slipped into the pier in San Francisco, the warmth
of my family's exuberant affection quickened my heart beat. Even in
the midst of all my excitement, I looked at the women around me with
an inner chuckle, for I thought of what Mrs. Knight had said about
walking up Market Street some day feeling dowdy. Well, she was
right. Two years had certainly made me out of date. The lovely tailored
suit I had worn, feeling so emancipated in the skirt four inches off the
ground, was now much too long, and there wasn't an Eton jacket in sight.

With my store of rich experiences, I was eager for an audience. I had
brought a little bag of high-grade dust from Goldfield, and with all
the skill of a seasoned prospector, I proudly panned dirt for my family
and friends, dramatically rolling the beautiful stuff around in the bottom of my mother's smallest frying pan. I had brought exquisite specimens of blistered high-grade from Goldfield, and I had a bit of ruby
silver from the Montana, which made lots of conversation until its
lovely color faded away.

For a month my mother and I had a wonderful time shopping in the morning and going to the theatre every possible afternoon — light opera, vaudeville, and best of all, *Camille,* with Madame Helena Modjeska. It was a rich experience to see that lovely, homely wonderful actress! All this entertainment and delightful activity, coupled with the affection my parents lavished upon me, sent me back to Tonopah refreshed and glowing.

Although construction on our house had continued all the time I was away, I knew it would not be anywhere near completion, for it was being built of adobe, not the adobe bricks the Mexicans have used for centuries, but adobe mud poured into troughs like concrete forms. Six months would be required to finish it, for each foot had to be allowed to dry before the next layer could be poured into the trough built up to receive it. The walls were eighteen inches thick, the windows flush with the outside walls. There was a layer of mud on the roof three inches thick. All this was designed to make the building impervious to winter winds and summer heat. The exterior was washed with a thin coat of grey paint, and the doors and window frames were stained dark brown. We moved in at Christmastime.

A glorious item in the new house was inside plumbing, which meant hot water! The water hole named Tonombe, fourteen miles to the north, proved to be an underground stream. This water was pumped to the surface and piped into town. Two high-pressure tanks on the hill behind our house furnished all Tonopah with running water. After two years we had no more use for the outhouse. What a relief! And now I no longer had to send my laundry on the three-week journey to Reno. The new house boasted two stationary tubs, and our new affluence furnished me with a fat little Negro girl who washed and ironed. Out of my own experience, I know hot running water is one of the most effective agencies of civilization.

Soon after we moved into our new home, Miss Eileen Higgins came to our town looking for material for a novel, which was called *The Little Princess of Tonopah.* She sent me a copy inscribed, "Perhaps you will see yourself as the 'Rainbow Lady,'" the bride whom the little girl visited. The writer gave a delightful description of the interior of our house, the walls covered with soft green grass cloth, the woodwork also green to comfort the eyes from the outside glare. She told about the mission-style furniture, the wedding gifts, the Chinese cook, and the geranium plants. Of course, Miss Higgins romanticized everything, but we were very pleased that she emphasized the elegance of our home.

A reception for Mrs. J. C. Campbell and her daughter was the first social affair in our new home. Apex litigation between two of the big mining companies brought Hugh's senior partner, Mr. Campbell, from San Francisco, and since no one ever missed an opportunity to visit our town, his wife and daughter came along. That reception was carried out with as much formality as it would have been in San Francisco, but with a difference. In the first place, the thirty guests taxed the capacity of the little house to its limits. The ladies were greeted by our Chinese servant and ushered quickly through the living room into our two-by-four library, where they were received by me and introduced to the guests of honor. Here the ladies lingered for a few moments and then drifted through the bathroom into the bedroom. The bed had been removed for the occasion, and all the chairs were assembled so that it was a very comfortable sitting room. Then the guests were ushered into the dining room by one of my friends. Here four card tables were set with all our lovely linen and silver, and decorated with a shaded candle in a small centerpiece of artificial flowers, which my mother had sent from San Francisco.

Now, why was all this maneuvering necessary? The living room was occupied by musicians! Where could one get musicians in Tonopah? From the Casino Dance Hall in the redlight district. I had violin, cello, and piano, under the leadership of Mr. Jules Goldsmith, an accomplished musician, eagle-visaged, dapper, and dark, with sleek black hair brushed up in a flat curl over his forehead in true gay-nineties fashion. He and his two assistants gave us music-starved women from "uptown" a rare treat. After listening to Mr. Goldsmith's music, we all declared we knew now that we really belonged "downtown."

The invaluable Fong served our guests chicken salad, coffee, and little cream tarts. Fong was an artist with a pastry bag and always eager to display his skill with curls and ruffles and whatnot, so I had tabulated the required number of C's and M's and S's in order that each guest might find her own initial on the top of her tart. Fong's artistry was received with gratifying enthusiasm and provided a fitting accent to a memorable occasion.

Amenities of city life that we thought were lost often turned up unexpectedly in Tonopah. One such surprise arrived at my door one day in the person of a young man carrying a milk jug. He offered me a glass of milk if I would supply him with a glass.

I could hardly credit what I heard, for a glass of milk on the desert was completely anachronistic. The man answered my expression of incredulity with a broad smile. He had brought in six fresh cows from

Inyo, California, and wanted to furnish fresh milk to us folks up on the hill. Would I give him a trial?

The milk was good, and he built quite a trade. It must have been an expensive operation, for all the fodder as well as the cows had to be hauled in by team. I used it for cooking and I drank it myself, but as it was not pasteurized I did not give it to my children.

Feeding our babies was something of a problem. My infants never had fresh milk at all. The first one was reared on malted milk and did pretty well, but as I look back with more experienced eyes, I know I took great chances. Young mothers of Tonopah had no pediatricians to advise them. We relied mostly on instinct and the trial-and-error method. When my second boy came along, I was more fortunate. I had an English doctor who, knowing nothing about American baby foods, induced me to send to England for a food called Allenbury's. The little fellow flourished on it.

That doctor was one of the most tragic figures we were to know in Tonopah. Dr. and Mrs. "Gable," as I shall call them, were very English, very charming, very entertaining. They lived among us for several years before the scandal from which they had fled crashed on their heads. Official inquiries came from England asking if a Dr. Gable was residing in Tonopah with a woman and a little boy. The doctor's wife in London was attempting to contact him to offer a divorce in exchange for custody of the boy. Although he was the child of the common-law wife, as the son of the doctor he was direct heir to a title. The doctor's legal wife proposed to adopt the boy and rear him as her own, a proposition that Dr. Gable rejected.

Gradually we learned that the doctor had been chief obstetrical surgeon in a large industrial hospital, a man of superb skill. He had fled from England with "the woman he loved" after their son was born, but he could not escape the inexorable laws of the social structure. After their story became common knowledge, the doctor's practice disappeared, and their gayety fell away. Mrs. Gable made no effort to keep alive the devotion of the man who had suffered disgrace for her, and the doctor took refuge in drugs. At last my husband and Tasker Oddie collected a few hundred dollars with which the pair left town. Later we heard that the doctor had died in some wretched roominghouse in San Francisco. What became of Mrs. Gable and the boy I never knew. My heart has carried a sympathetic ache for these two in their disgrace and lonely death far from home.

Of the few doctors who were in Tonopah, I think the only one who

Mining towns attract fascinating people. Mrs. Key Pittman, shown here in her parlor, once drove a dog team over the Yukon Trail in midwinter—alone! Later, when her husband was elected to the U. S. Senate, she became one of Washington's favorite hostesses. (Her friends in Dawson thought it took more courage to marry the soldier of fortune from Mississippi than to brave the Yukon Trail.)

Desert entertaining was lavish, if a bit make-do. This dinner party
in the Merchants Hotel was given by Charles Knox (far left), president of
the Montana-Tonopah Mining Company. We had cactus for centerpieces and
beer mugs for goblets, but our host managed fresh strawberries,
plenty of champagne, and favors for the ladies—"assayer's buttons" of pure silver.

Our little circle of ladies met on Mondays, so Mrs. Key Pittman
suggested we call ourselves the "Lunas Clava."
The name stuck, even after we discovered that "clava"
meant a much more dangerous kind of club!

In Goldfield every other building was a saloon and gambling house. Men in high boots and wide felt hats crowded around the tables to toss ten- and twenty-dollar gold pieces for one turn of the wheel. Six-shooters were often in evidence.

Dance-hall girls in Tonopah looked somewhat different from their TV counterparts. Their companion here is Walter Drysdale, resplendent in bow tie and high button shoes. Walter achieved local fame on the other side of the bar, as a "mixologist."

Where in Tonopah could you hire musicians? At the dance halls down in the redlight. Jules Goldsmith and his assistants (shown here on stage at the Big Casino) once gave my music-starved guests from "uptown" a rare treat.

The Butler Theatre offered marvels of gay-nineties entertainment. The prima donna (center) sang such popular songs as "Wouldn't You Like to See a Little More of Me?" and "How about a Little Lovin'?" One night the cartoonist for the Tonopah Sun decided to accept her invitation. He jumped onto the stage and planted a kiss squarely on her painted mouth. But when he followed her into the wings, she swung hard and sent him flying back onto the stage.

Baseball was a big thing in Tonopah. There were several local teams, including this one from the Pullman Club.

The Elks nine and rooters look harmless enough here, but rivalries were fierce and games often ended in fist fights.

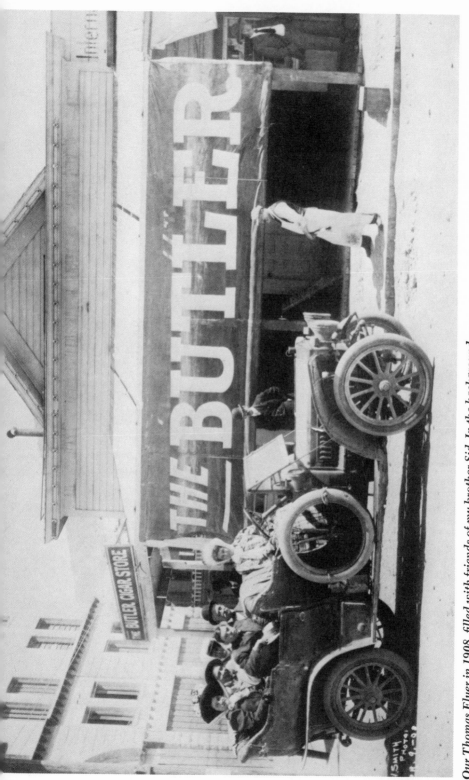

Our Thomas Flyer in 1908, filled with friends of my brother Sid. In the background is the Butler Theatre, which became a burlesque house two years later. The man in the apron is a candymaker of whom we were all very fond.

An auto excursion to Goldfield. With heat and flash floods in summer, blizzards in winter, and boulder-strewn roads year-round, motoring across the desert was a real adventure. Man at right is Key Pittman.

A jolly group of Sunday sharpshooters take aim for the photographer. (I am standing, second from left.)

After the shoot, a picnic. In mild weather we often spent Sunday afternoons this way.

*Fourth of July, 1912. The boom had ended, but the parades went on.
Little Hugh is the page with the big white feather.*

The patriotic fervor of World War I swept all the way to Nevada. Tanks were new and a curiosity, so the government sent this one to Tonopah for a Liberty Loan drive. I had the questionable privilege of riding in it—up mountainsides, down mine craters, bouncing around in the turret.

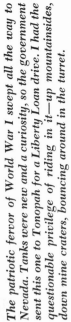

When California women adopted riding breeches for motoring, I did too. I was criticized by other women, but I don't think the men minded at all. One told me years later, "You looked like a handsome boy!"

1918, and Tonopah still paraded. My group of Junior Red Cross girls decorated this truck with sagebrush, showing as much enthusiasm as their parents had for the first Railroad Days. But the early excitement was over, and times were changing.

came for the professional experience the camp offered was Dr. P. D. McLeod. Long before the time when two world wars challenged surgeons to salvage mutilated men, Dr. McLeod was interested in repairing the bodies of men injured in mine accidents.

Doctors who came to Tonopah had a way of attracting gossip. One, so it was whispered, was a drug addict in Alaska; one was said to have fled from the publicity of a murder trial in which he had been accused of being an accessory after the fact, assisting in the disposal of the body. Another was a dashing, handsome soldier of fortune, who died of blood poisoning. Gossip on the street reported he had cut his finger while operating. When his nurse pulled off the punctured glove, he said to her, "I'll be dead in a week."

"Just as if he was looking for a way to die," she was reported to have said. I can't vouch for this story, but I do know that in a very short time the doctor was certainly dead.

Beside being one of the first women in town to buy fresh milk, I was definitely the first to have a vacuum cleaner. Sometime along in the early years, I chanced upon a three-line ad in a copy of the Sunday *New York Times* announcing a "mechanical sweeper." In Tonopah, the constant struggle with the talcum-like dust was a trial to all of us, so the ad caught my interest.

I replied, sending along the twenty-five dollars requested.

When the machine was finally delivered, Hugh recognized its likeness to the Butters filter in use at the Belmont mill. Charles Butters, a distinguished metallurgist from California, had only recently developed this filter to complement a cyanide formula. My sweeper acted with the dust exactly as the Butters filter acted with the mud from the cyanide-silver solution. The dust, like the muddy solution, was drawn into the vacuum chamber by the hand pump, and just as the mud adhered to the big filters when the silver-impregnated solution was pumped through, so the dust stuck to the little filters in the sweeper. The way that machine sucked the fine dust out of my carpets was glorious! We made a social event of cleaning the filters, calling in our neighbors to view the marvel and wager on the volume of dust that would be extracted.

Later we learned the promoters were two former mill hands from Goldfield, who had indeed borrowed the idea from the Butters filter. We were also told that they cleaned up a neat fortune before Charles Butters' lawyers and prison caught up with them on charges of patent infringements.

Today we take our luxuries so much for granted: vacuum cleaners, refrigeration, inspected milk, and so on; yet it was hardly more than yesterday that young women were wrestling with relatively primitive conditions.

Tonopah had three disastrous fires during my life there. I was personally somewhat involved with the first one. The birth of our second son was approaching, and I lay in bed one night timing the rapidity of my pains, wondering if I ought to alert the family. Suddenly I heard the fire whistle, a terrifying sound in the night. Hugh ascertained that the fire was in a big miners' boardinghouse across town called "The Ship." An hour later, when Hugh thought it was time to telephone our doctor that we needed him, he was told that the doctor had been called to the hospital to care for those who had been hurt. As the night advanced, this situation became of real concern to us. Ultimately the doctor did arrive, and not any too soon. No mention was made of the tragedy on the other side of town.

The second fire was a holocaust. One winter morning the news spread through the town as if by telepathy: "Fire in the Belmont!" Clouds of dense smoke were billowing from the mine shaft, precluding any possibility of rescue, and the lives of seventeen men were snuffed out. It was surmised that some miner had left a burning candle that ultimately ignited the timber on which it was resting.

Tonopah declared a week of mourning. The caskets lay in state in the Miners' Union Headquarters, surrounded by a guard of honor. Hundreds of miners arrived from nearby camps. With drums muffled and flags furled in black crepe, they walked behind trucks bearing the caskets through driving sleet to the drab little cemetery at the end of Main Street.

We had two regular newspapers in Tonopah. The Tonopah *Sun* was edited by L. C. Branson, a cold, hard man I could never get close to; but I had a real affection for the rough-diamond qualities of Bill Booth, who edited the rival daily, the Tonopah *Bonanza*. When I had causes to defend, I went to Bill Booth, and I always got a square deal from his paper.

Arthur Buel was a cartoonist on the Tonopah *Sun,* a really good artist. He drew remarkably fine portraits of our leading citizens as well as delightful cartoons, his signature for which was a little burro. Arthur himself was a character right out of Bret Harte, with a big lumbering body and a heart as big. No "fancy pants," he liked those quiet little evenings when the boys got to fogging around the saloons.

I have a vivid memory of one of Arthur's escapades. During the camp's later and more "respectable" years, the Butler saloon was turned into a small theatre. One troupe of traveling actors presented a show that was a marvel of gay-nineties entertainment, with women of uncertain age dressed as babies, and real stunt men and comedians. The prima donna was a large, florid woman with a big pompadour and wasp waist, who sang such popular songs of the period as "Wouldn't You Like to See a Little More of Me?" and "How About a Little Lovin'."

One night Arthur Buel decided to accept her invitation. As she leered down at him from the stage, he clambered over the seats, stepped from the piano onto the stage, grabbed her, and planted a manly kiss squarely on her painted mouth. Indignant, she pushed him away and marched off the stage, with Arthur in pursuit. Suddenly there was a loud smack, and Arthur came flying out on the stage, rubbing his cheek. Amid howls of laughter from all of us, he climbed down over the piano again and made sheepishly for his seat.

Twenty years later he came to my home in California with a carload of family — the same smiling, rollicking Arthur Buel, just bigger and shaggier, that was all. I was so glad to see him, I hugged him, and Mrs. Buel stood by with an expression that plainly said, "Oh, I'm used to that. Everybody loves my husband."

As the years passed, we hired an assortment of different people to assist with the housekeeping, among them two wonderful Chinese boys and a Bavarian woman who had been a saloonkeeper in Rhyolite, but was an excellent cook. However, she hadn't been with us for more than a few months before we discovered that she was lifting the fancy canned goods we imported from "outside" and was selling them to the girls in the redlight. Another of the heterogeneous mass of humanity who drifted out to the frontier for reasons of their own was a Chautauqua lecturer, very much on her uppers. I never discovered how good a lecturer she was, but I soon found out she knew nothing about cooking.

An "unforgettable character" was an elderly Negro woman named Carrie. It is with a feeling of atonement that I offer here a tribute to her gentle spirit. Like the others, Carrie answered my ad in the Tonopah *Bonanza*. When I saw her at the front door, I was sure she would not do. She was tall and gaunt and homely as a giraffe. But my third child was about to arrive, and Carrie assured me that she was a "good old-fashioned cook," so I engaged her.

That evening, as Carrie came into the dining room to remove the plates before serving dessert, I looked at the lean, spider like body with its blue gingham apron and was sure I could never make up my mind to look at it day after endless day. The apron could be changed, but what could change that frame? However, the dinner was well cooked, and I discovered that Carrie made excellent bread —surely a boon out here!

In order to improve her appearance, I sent to San Francisco for the largest black maid's uniforms I could buy, together with white nurse's aprons, the kind with bibs and full skirts that would be all-enveloping. Of course, when the clothes arrived, they were very much too big for her slat-like body, but they were long enough. I got out my treasured little Wilcox and Gibbs sewing machine and took in the seams until the dress fit. Carrie was as pleased as a child with the new clothes, and when I saw her completely dressed, I was delighted. She had smoothed back her thin grey hair, and the white cuffs on the uniforms took the curse off those long bony fingers.

But Carrie's idea of housekeeping was not commensurate with her cooking. I would chide her for the careless way the silverware was thrown on the table, or complain of the spotted tablecloth that should not have been used again; and she would serve us some little extra treat for lunch, such as corn bread or popovers, for a sort of peace offering.

One afternoon I heard Carrie's slow step coming toward the library, where I was sitting with my younger son. She stopped hesitantly in the doorway and said, "Mrs. Brown, kin I talk to you a minute?"

"Certainly, Carrie. Sit down."

"No," she replied, in her soft southern voice. "I'll just stand here." After a pause, she continued, "I know I don't suit you, but I thought maybe if I knowed what I done wrong, maybe I could do better. I want to please you."

"But, Carrie," I said, "I do tell you over and over again, and you forget. It's just so many things. I don't know where to begin." She looked down for a moment and smoothed out her white apron with her two big hands and said gently:

"Well, then I'll go. I just does the best I knows how."

Needless to say, she didn't leave me in my need. Carrie stayed until my baby girl was well launched, and then she drifted out of our lives. In the many years since this humble, faithful soul crossed my path, when life has pressed me hard, I've remembered the look on her gentle, homely face. Her words have been a call to me to "go and do likewise" —"I just does the best I knows how."

And then came Mrs. Margaret Donald —"Donnie," a darling middle-class Scottish widow. Lonely in San Francisco because her only daughter was living in Canada, she wanted a position in a house where she could be one of the family. She sat with us at table, and our friends were hers. She was a "housekeeper," but she was a guardian angel and a beloved member of our family for many years.

At last Donnie was enticed away from us by the county commissioners, who insisted they needed her warmth and efficiency as matron at the County Hospital. In this position, she had many interesting contacts, like the one with Jack Longstreet, the man who tangled with Tasker Oddie over a claim-jumping accusation in the early days. Incidentally, he was reported to be a near relative of General James Longstreet of Civil War fame. He was a big, muscular man with grey hair, which he wore over-long. He was supposed to have lost one ear, cut off for horse-stealing when he was a youth. Nobody knew for certain whether that ear was off and it would have been as much as anyone's life was worth to try to find out. But while Donnie was at the County Hospital, she told me this story: "The old man came in pretty sick. We got him into bed, I brought a basin of water and soap. You know how it is, it's just routine with us. Everybody gets washed when they are brought in dirty from the hills. I washed off his face, and then I pushed away his hair to get at his ears. Well! he slapped my hand down, sick as he was. His arm flashed out quick as a gun. I pretty near fainted!"

Donnie paused and I asked breathlessly, "Was the ear off?"

"It was off!" she said impressively. "And he swore at me a blue streak. 'All right,' I says, 'all right. You can stay dirty for all I care.' But he yelled at me, 'You keep your blankety-blank hands offa me, and if you talk about me, I'll kill ya!' And believe me, I didn't say anything about that ear bein' off until I knew he was good and dead. I hope the old fellow don't haunt me for telling you about him now."

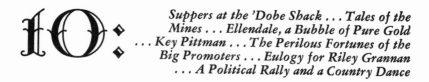

THE " 'DOBE SHACK," as we lovingly called our home, became the center and circumference of our lives. This was not surprising, since there was so little by way of entertainment outside our homes, even Tasker's horses were gone as soon as the railroad arrived, so we made a practice of giving Sunday night suppers to which our friends were bidden without special invitation. We bought beer by the barrel, cheese by the wheel, crackers and canned goods by the case; and for years I had a special type of nightmare wherein I rummaged endlessly for food through kitchen and cellar, because we had a houseful of men and nothing to feed them.

We would sit around the table until midnight, swapping yarns, reporting strikes, talking local politics. My father would have thought we were very provincial, for I can't remember talking about anything of national importance, except, of course, such items as Will Rogers' appearance in 1905, with his lariat, at the horseshow in Madison Square Garden; or perhaps Maud Adams as Peter Pan imploring her audiences to "believe in fairies" and save the life of Tinker Bell; or Teddy Roosevelt telling his countrymen to "speak softly and carry a big stick."

Southern Nevada mines had brought prosperity to all of us, and we had real drama to talk about — personal drama about people we knew. We delighted in stories of good fortune, like the discovery of Ellendale.

Jim Clifford, the man who figured in Tasker's run-in with Jack Longstreet, together with his wife Ellen, had roamed the desert examining every "likely-lookin' piece of rock." No doubt it was the lost Breyfogel they were seeking, or some other of the many rich finds, uncharted because the original discoverer could not return to the spot again, or died on the desert, or was killed by Indians. Southern Nevada was completely untracked. Barstow was only a fueling point for the Santa Fe engines, and Las Vegas was hardly more than a Mexican village. One day, with her prospector's hammer, Mrs. Clifford cracked open a boulder and laid bare a thrilling piece of leaf gold. Then for weeks she and her husband searched the surrounding country until they traced the ledge from which the piece of float had rolled. They named the spot "Ellendale," and in no time at all, claims were staked out for miles around, a town was laid out, and lots auctioned off for high figures.

Hugh and I never missed the excitement of a discovery, so one Sunday we went out to see Ellendale. The Cliffords had dug out a shallow hole; we slipped down into it and saw a face of pure leaf gold, which I touched with a finger. One flake came off in my hand. "Hey!" said Hugh. "Stop robbing the Clifford's jewelry store."

This ore was far more spectacular than Goldfield's, where the ore had to be subjected to intense heat before little blisters of pure gold appeared. At the time we were there, the Cliffords had sixty sacks of high-grade ore stacked in a little shed, each sack worth $1,000. Ellendale proved to be a bubble of almost pure gold, which, through some freak of nature, had been thrust to the surface. However, the first shot of powder they put in to dig a shaft blew all the values away. It was not an entire loss, for they had the $60,000, but the mine and townsite never materialized.

Key Pittman was another one who had a rare stroke of luck. He came to Tonopah from Alaska, where he had not made a fortune, nor did he have a winning lease in Goldfield. But down on the flat in Tonopah district was a mine that became flooded with water and was forced into bankruptcy. As the company lawyer, Key was the principal creditor. Much to his regret, he had to accept the property in lieu of a fee. Figuring he was probably sending good money after bad, he decided to risk a few hundred dollars to estimate the worth of the fee. He installed pumps to lower the water level and put on three shifts of men to explore the old shaft. A few hundred feet deeper and, yes, they encountered a vein that made Key Pittman rich. The next step was the United States Senate.

During his stay in the far North, Key had been the first district attorney of Dawson, Yukon Territory, and had tried to curb corruption among government officials. He was a tall, pale, slender sapling, a hard drinker, and when intoxicated belligerent to the point of endangering his own life as well as the lives of others. While he was in Dawson, he married Miss Mimosa Gates, who was something of a celebrity in her own right. She had made an impressive journey by dog team down the Yukon trail from Dawson to Juneau, an unbelievable feat if you look at the map. Her adventurous spirit captured the imagination of the soldier of fortune from Mississippi, but I was told by someone who had known her in Dawson that her friends thought it took more courage for her to marry Key Pittman than to face the Yukon trail. Be that as it may, to the very end of his life she was the only one who could control him when he went off the deep end. They were a glamorous pair.

How fortune smiled at some and passed up others was a yarn that was always cropping up. Hugh told me an interesting story about the man who built the Golden Block, the little white building where Hugh had his office.

Frank Golden was an itinerant jeweler who thumbed a ride into Tonopah with a freighter. He had a valise full of cufflinks, watches, and stick pins to sell to the leasers. He ran into a man who had a lease that didn't seem likely to pan out. Golden offered him a watch in exchange for the lease, and the deal was closed. Golden put two men to work on the cut while he opened a little hole-in-the-wall jewelry shop on Main Street near the Merchants' Hotel. They broke into ore just beyond where the vein had faulted, and Frank Golden netted $500,000.

He thought it would be nice to put up "the first permanent building" in Tonopah, but there wasn't anything around to build with. Then he noticed a patch of white stone showing behind where our house now was. He discovered that it was soft and easy to quarry, and that it hardened when it was exposed to the air. So he put up the little building—a good job, too, tight and warm. Then he went to Reno and built the Golden Hotel, where we stayed the night we came into Reno on our honeymoon.

Zeb Kendall, the "big promoter" who had been one of our traveling companions on the stage to Tonopah, was another whose mercurial fortunes often came up for discussion around our Sunday night supper table. Probably the most dynamic men of the camp, the promoters never prospected but always knew where money could be flushed out to option any "likely lookin'" spot of ground. They were intelligent, usually educated, and well dressed.

Zeb loved the little brown-eyed girl who had been queen of the Railroad Days parade, Belle Pepper; he hovered over her like a Newfoundland over a kitten. I think her woman's intuition warned her that she would have a precarious life if she married him. Zeb played for high stakes over the table as well as underground, but ultimately, Belle did marry him and followed him through one fortune after another. Once, when I knew he was "in the money," I told him that he ought to buy his wife an annuity so that she and the boys would be safe no matter what happened to him. "Oh, I do," he said, rubbing the side of his face with the flat of his hand, a characteristic mannerism. "Every time I make a stake, I always put money away for her, but I always get to needing it and have to borrow it back."

Zeb and Belle had a son who was born on Abraham Lincoln's centenary. Zeb was in the Nevada State Senate at the time, and the legislature passed a bill naming the boy Abraham Lincoln Kendall. His mother was furious. She said to me, "I don't want the boy called '*Abe*' all his life!" But there was nothing she could do about it; it was a law.

Exciting as were the reports of new strikes, it was the anecdotes about high finance that really provided thrills.

One of our guests told us that the money poured in so fast, they were ashamed to take it to the bank. A hundred thousand dollars in one day. They kept it in an old rolltop desk, and sat up all night with their feet cocked up against it so they'd look casual and discourage a hold-up. "And, by God," our friend said, "I nearly landed in jail. Some fellows were selling stock in ground they knew was worthless, but we had no intention of doing anything crooked. The money just rolled over us, like a wave we couldn't stop."

Whether by more experienced or less innocent manipulations, we knew of companies incorporated by New York financiers on ground that they knew had no value. The stock was issued and put on the market. Usually the prospector who had sold the claims got a block of stock "held in pool"— that is, not to be sold until a certain date. But before the date arrived, the prospector would be offered, say fifty cents a share by the "big shot" in New York. To the man who had lived on bacon and beans most of his life, this was a fortune — fifteen thousand dollars, maybe twenty thousand dollars. And he'd sell. In the meantime, the stock that had started at eight cents on the mining exchange would be pushing a dollar. By the time the pool was broken, the stock might be selling for two dollars. Then the "big shot" with a hundred thousand shares would begin to unload. The stock would go down, down, down.

Among those whose names recurred in our conversations from time to time was Herman Knickerbocker, sometimes minister, Shakespearean reader, prospector, and gambler. Ultimately, as the years went on, Mr. Knickerbocker's luck deserted him and he began to roam the state following each new strike. At last, at Rawhide, he made a famous oration over the body of Riley Grannan that brought his name to the attention of the whole country.

Rawhide was a mining strike about a hundred miles northwest of Tonopah, one of many that swept the state in the backwash of Goldfield's tidal wave. Here Riley Grannan, a fabulous character known as race-track plunger, big-time gambler and sport extraordinary, had opened a gambling house. Rawhide never had enough ore at any time to justify a townsite; consequently roulette and blackjack were the sole occupations of the camp followers who drifted from one strike to the next as each new location appeared.

One stormy, snow-drenched night, after a six-hour session of poker, Riley Grannan, in his shirtsleeves, walked out of his saloon into the cold night air. The result? Pneumonia. In a few days Riley Grannan was dead. Though there was no church in Rawhide and no hearse, all the people to whom Riley had given money and food and whiskey and a pat on the back when they were down on their luck insisted he must have a grand funeral. So the body, in its pine box, was hauled on an ore wagon to Riley's saloon and there laid out in front of the bar, while his friends grouped themselves around the gambling tables.

Here, extemporaneously, Mr. Knickerbocker delivered a funeral oration rarely equalled for deep feeling and genuine philosophy, and it would have been lost to all but his hearers had it not been for the presence of a newspaperman from California. Luckily the newsman was a shorthand expert, and he transcribed the words as they fell from Knickerbocker's mouth. That night, with no revision, he sent a copy to the Reno *Gazette*; the oration was headlined the following night and was flashed to the world.

"He lived in the world of sport. I do not mince my words, I am telling what I believe to be true. In the world of sport, hilarity sometimes, and maybe worse. He left the impress of his character on this world, and through the medium of his financial power, he was able with his money to brighten the lives of its inhabitants. He wasted it, so the world says. But did it ever occur to you that the most sinful men and women who live in this world are still men and women? Did it ever occur to you that the men and women who inhabit the night-world are still men and women? A little happiness brought into their lives means as much to them as happiness brought into the lives of the straight and good. If you can take one ray of sunlight into their night-life and thereby bring them one single hour of happiness, I believe you are a benefactor . . ."

It took one dramatic outcast to pay fitting tribute to another dramatic outcast.

Among the friends who gathered at our house on Sunday night were some wonderful storytellers. King of them all was Dick Dunlap. One night the men were talking about the ease and rapidity with which claims changed hands and how necessary it was to close a deal at once lest it evaporate before morning. Dick told us of a conversation he had had with Cal Brougher: " 'Cal', I said, 'do you want that fraction out at Divide I told you about?' Cal said, 'Sure. How much do you want for it?' I said, 'Five thousand dollars.' Cal took out his billfold and scanned it carefully. 'I haven't got that much on me, Dick. Will you wait until tomorrow morning?' "

And here is Dick's story of a conversation between two old-timers: One was going to New York, and wanted to see Chris Zabriski. (Chris was a native Nevadan who, as a boy, had been a telegrapher in Candelaria. When Borax Smith ran into his mountain of borax in Death Valley Chris Zabriski was his right-hand man. He rose with the Twenty-Mule Team Borax Company to be general manager, with headquarters in New York — a lovable, gregarious fellow. Chris had a host of friends in the state, all of whom he welcomed in New York at any time and in any number.)

One old desert rat said to the other, "Pete, I'm going to New York. How do I git to see Chris Zabriski?"

"Goin' to New York, eh? Well, Chris always likes to see any old horn toad from Nevada, and he knows every saloonkeeper from the Battery to the Bronx. He'll see you git a snootful any time, day or night."

"Well, how will I find him?"

"He's in a dump they call the Empire Building. You take the hoist to the tenth level, then take the first crosscut to the east, and you'll see his location notice on the door."

But Dick was also given to the fast quip. I had tried the cream tart stunt one night, and didn't have all the letters necessary. "I just haven't tarts enough to go around," I remarked ruefully as I passed the plate of dessert. Quick as a flash, Dick turned to the man next to him.

"Say," he said, "were you ever at a party where there were enough tarts?"

We never knew what kind of an adventure story was going to be told around our table on Sunday evening, or what new experience would come of the stranger brought along by one of our guests. One of the most delightful surprises happened the night Charles Knox brought with him Mr. Parkhurst, an officer in the Montana Company. After supper Mr. Parkhurst sat down at the piano and played softly while the others were still chatting at the table. I sat nearby, raptly listening. At last he turned to me and asked me about the plans we ladies were making for a library. I was surprised at his remark, for the idea was so new I did not expect anyone to mention it. But I explained to him that there was no place in town where the miners could go except the saloons. Mr. Parkhurst wondered if they wanted to go anywhere else. "If they had a room uptown where they could go and read quietly, they would use it," I replied. We ladies were sure they would.

Mr. Knox came over from the table and joined us. He said that he had been mulling the idea over in his mind since he had first heard of it. He thought that every man who could be encouraged to patronize such a room would be just that much less grief for the mine operators and would keep some of his money in his own pocket. He thought the operators ought to help. Mr. Parkhurst agreed and, turning back to me, promised to give us five hundred dollars.

"I'll do more than that," added Mr. Knox, "I'll take it up with the Mine Operators' Association and see if we can't give you a lot to build a cabin on."

A few days later, I received a letter from Mr. Knox enclosing a check for a thousand dollars and a deed to a lot on Mineral Street. With this boost for our enthusiasm, we plunged ahead, first with a book social, then with a minstrel show at the Opera House and other festivities until we had enough money to put up a beautiful little stone building. There we gathered several thousand volumes, as well as subscriptions to a few newspapers and magazines. The library was a great addition to the town and was used by everyone. I look back with real happiness to the creation of that little building. It was as near as I ever came to experiencing Al Meyer's opportunity to create something soul-satisfying.

Of our personal friends, the most romantic figure was Herman Albert. He was associated with Reese River, a bright spot in my memory book. Herman came to Tonopah in 1903, directly after his graduation from Columbia University, a trimly built young man with fine eyes and an exceptionally sweet smile. He was a natural musician, who only a few months before had written the music for the senior opera at his alma mater. It was so tuneful that it was moved from Columbia's campus directly to Broadway.

But Herman had a wanderlust, and after a few months in Tonopah, he plunged still deeper into the life of the West with a string of burros and a package of bacon and beans. When he returned from his prospecting trips, he never had anything to show except a beard that made him look like the apostle Paul. He would stay in town for a few weeks and occasionally come up on the hill to play the piano; then civilization, such as it was, irked him, and he was gone again.

At last Herman attached himself to the George Keough ranch at Reese River, where the families of the Bells and the Keoughs lived like patriarchs of old. Their cattle ranches stretched for hundreds of miles on both sides of the old river bed from which the district drew its name.

Political spokesmen from Tonopah always went to outlying districts to hold rallies. I discovered early that one of these trips could be a wonderful holiday. During one sensational campaign, Hugh went to Reese River to address the voters in behalf of Key Pittman's opponent. We were "put up" at the Bell ranch, and the meeting was held in the district schoolhouse — followed, of course, by an all-night dance.

The schoolhouse was the usual white-board, one-room structure, with a hitching rail across the length of the building; off to the right were a well and a watering trough. Inside, a piano and rows of benches were arranged for the political rally. To me the meeting seemed undistinguished, even if Hugh was making the speech; it was the audience that captivated me: weatherworn cowboys; rugged, substantial-looking ranchers; mothers of ample proportions with soft eyes and hard hands, whose manners were diffident but not uncordial; young girls with frizzed hair and frilled dresses, interested only in the cowboys from the distant ranches; young men of all ages in overalls, with sleek heads and sunburned noses. And outside, brown faces of Indians banked the three windows on each side of the room.

After the speeches the benches were pushed back against the wall. Little children were induced to relinquish the soft side of Dad's arm and lie down on the hard benches with sweaters for pillows. At last a woman in a white dress sat down at the piano, a young man came forward with a violin, and the dance began. One-two-three, one-two-three, the fiddler played, but without the vestige of a tune, while the lady at the piano never once changed her two chords.

Because this was an all-night function, a program had been arranged to take care of the intermissions. Herman Albert was master of ceremonies. A middle-aged rancher sang a bass solo in a rich, strong voice; Miss Virginia Somebody recited "Barbara Fritchie"; Mr. and Mrs. So-and-So played a duet while Herman made the announcements in the tones of a benevolent parent.

When midnight arrived, we drank strong coffee brewed in a cauldron hung on a crane over the great fire out in the school yard, with Indians of all ages gathered around for their share. We ate sandwiches of homemade bread, home-cured ham, and cakes such as only ranch women can make; thus fortified, we danced until the clouds turned pink. Then we rode back up the lane to the Bell ranch five miles away and had breakfast before we went to bed.

How we happened to be entertained at the Bell ranch is a story in itself. We were to have been guests at the Keough ranch, a staunch Republican citadel; but on the afternoon of our arrival, found Mrs. Keough was ill, so we rode back ten miles to the Bell ranch. We felt quite uncomfortable about storming unannounced into this Democratic stronghold, but we were received by Senator Bell and his family with as much graciousness as if we had been members of his own political party. This in itself was a commentary on desert hospitality, for old Nevadans took their politics seriously. We found out they took their hospitality even more seriously.

Because we had come to attend a Republican rally, our party manager thought it only right to offer to pay for our lodging. When the suggestion was made to the senator, he drew himself up, every white hair bristling, his face drained of color, and said in a quiet voice, "You insult me, sir. You were my guests."

Turning on his heel, he walked to the door and out into the yard, where he leaned against a cottonwood, looking far off over the field where his thousand head of cattle stood lazily in the hot sun. The moment was terrible. The quiet anger in that old man's figure was a lesson in outraged hospitality I have never forgotten.

At last Hugh walked over and spoke to him; the senator's handsome features relaxed. The party manager went forward, extending his hand in apology. Mr. Bell shook it warmly, and the incident was over.

San Francisco . . . April 18, "A Violent Heaving and Shaking!". . . The Scene at the Palace . . . A Refugee in Black Lace and Feathers . . . Curb-Side Cookout on Nob Hill . . . A Lost Layette and Greater Tragedies . . . Riding an Express Wagon Through the Smoking Ruins

IN 1906 TONOPAH WAS AT THE HEIGHT of its productivity and Goldfield at the apex of its boom; new discoveries were being made all over southern Nevada, and money was flowing through our hands like water. There was a steady stream of business in Hugh's office, as he helped promoters of new mining ventures to launch their companies. As these new strikes kept rolling in, his fees were often paid in stock in the new companies rather than money. Every new company was listed on the stock exchange almost overnight, with their potential as producers rising with every market day. These were the top of the boom days, for us as well as for the promoters.

Our first child was about to be born, and we had much to celebrate. We had planned that I should be with my mother through my confinement, so we went to San Francisco a few weeks early to take in the opera season. Though I had visited my family the previous autumn, I was tremendously thrilled over this trip. As a girl, when I sat in the balcony or, more probably, stood on the ground floor to hear Melba and Sembrick, Schumann-Heink and other brilliant stars clustered around the 1890's, I had dreamed of such luxury. Now it was here. Our tickets were ordered and received, tenth row on the aisle, and my mother was commissioned to have an appropriate dress ready for me when the date came.

We arrived in the city early on Monday morning, April 16. Like loyal Nevadans, we went to the Palace Hotel, which had been built with Nevada mining money. We were settled in an attractive, old-fashioned corner room on the fifth floor, with long green and gold draperies with valances and fringe, and chairs upholstered in gold brocade. A huge fireplace with carved marble mantel, surmounted by a large mirror in a fluted gold frame, practically filled one side of the room. It was the handsomest room either of us had ever occupied.

That afternoon we both went shopping for clothes. Anticipating my expanding figure, my mother had had made for me a light blue evening gown to wear at the opera, but I needed an evening wrap. I bought a beautiful grey one trimmed with fur, and Hugh laid in a whole new outfit.

Late Monday afternoon our purchases were delivered to the hotel by messenger; Hugh's wardrobe came stacked in two tiers of six boxes each, with handles on top by which the boy carried them: new suits, shirts, ties, socks, a complete wardrobe. My own new clothes would materialize after our child was born.

I have not the slightest recollection of what opera we heard that first night. The excitement of the day, the beautiful hotel room, the new clothes, with Hugh so handsome in his dress suit and top hat, drove everything else out of my mind. But the following night Caruso, at the top of his career, sang *Carmen*! To this moment, I can hear his honeyed voice with its strange pathos soaring through the high vaulted ceiling of the Morosko Opera House.

After the performance we returned quickly to the hotel, for we had invited a half-dozen Tonopah friends to join us for supper in the Palm Court. The gayly ornamented room was crowded with richly dressed men and women, while from the eight crystal-chandeliered galleries above, people looked down on the brilliant scene.

Judge Jackson was one of our guests that night, and in the course of conversation he reminded me of the remark he had made that night in Goldfield about our making a hundred thousand dollars. I interrupted him, "And didn't I tell you we'd make three times that amount?"

He smiled understandingly. "Yes," he said, "and I guess you will."

We were among the last to leave the Palm Court that night. Hugh and I went up in the elevator to our room, feeling life could add nothing more to our happiness. We walked through the wide, red-carpeted halls, eloquent of the grandeur of an earlier day; now another Nevada boom was on and we were part of it! I slipped off my pretty blue dress and laid it carefully over the big upholstered chair. After our full day, sleep came easily and quickly.

Suddenly I was awakened by a strange rumbling that grew louder and angrier as it came nearer, culminating in a violent heaving and shaking. Then the terrifying sound of breaking glass followed, and plaster and soot showered down on us. In terror, I clutched my husband. He kept saying, as he leaned over me protectingly, "It's all right, dear! It's all right!"

I knew what it was. I had been born in San Francisco. An earthquake—a terrible one! Then came that ghastly few minutes of stillness. I have read a great deal about people's impressions of the shock, but no one seems to have recorded the seemingly interminable moment of stillness that followed it. Then little sounds began, swelling fast to the noise and confusion of rushing feet out in the hall.

We slipped out of bed and looked through the jagged glass of our windows to the big plate glass frames of the Southern Pacific offices opposite. They were empty holes. Down on the street lay piles of shattered fragments, together with countless bricks that seemed to have rained from the sky. In the softness of the early morning light, I stood there long enough to take in the scene. Then I began to totter and Hugh led me back to bed. Now we began to assess our own immediate surroundings. The air was filled with soot and plaster, and the floor was inches deep with black and white debris, together with the glass from the big mirror above the mantel, every few minutes another brick came hurtling down the chimney, sending clouds of soot into the room, covering everything, including my lovely blue dress.

Hugh took the counterpane off the bed and draped it over the fireplace to keep the soot from pouring in; then, with the top of the box in which my wrap had been delivered, he swept glass and plaster into a corner so he could move about the room with some degree of safety.

With returning awareness, my first thought was for my mother and father in the family home, an old frame house on Taylor Street near Washington. Had I known it, they could not have been in a safer situation, as the old wooden houses stood the shake with elastic fortitude; but now in my imagination, my parents lay pinned in their beds under the wreckage of the old structure.

Hugh tried to comfort me, but for an hour I wept with anxiety. Then I thought I heard a voice calling as if out of a dream,"I'm looking for Mrs. Hugh Brown! *I'm looking for Mrs. Hugh Brown!"*

My sister! Never have I heard anything so exquisite as her high, sweet voice calling my name above the din of shouts and scuffling feet. Hugh opened the door to Mary Belle and her little four-year-old daughter. We fell into each other's arms.

My parents were safe, as was every member of the family. As quickly as my sister could get herself together after the shock, she took her little girl and ran most of the mile from her own home to my parents! Finding them unharmed, she continued down the hill to the Palace Hotel to find me. The anxiety of the whole family was centered on me, with the birth of our child so near.

Mary Belle told us of the chaos downstairs in the lobby. Even in these trying circumstances, she had to take time out to laugh over the ludicrous sights she had seen: the man in dress coat and vest and no trousers, only long underwear; the woman in curl papers and flowing negligee, hugging a dog to her bosom as she clattered around in mules seeking coffee.

Then Mary Belle went to the hotel roof for a better view of the disaster. Rushing back with eyes full of terror, she reported that already three big fires were well underway, one of them at the Grand Opera House, very close to the Palace Hotel. We must leave at once.

It wasn't easy to get into my clothes, but I did manage a maternity dress of black silk. Then I looked over my hats. I chose the black lace with feathers, the one I had worn to Tom Lynch's wedding. It was utterly inappropriate, but it was the handsomest, so I thought it ought to be saved.

By the time we were ready for the street, my mother had arrived. My sister felt she could leave us and attend to her own troubled situation, intending to meet us at our home later in the day. As she departed, she promised to take care of my baby clothes and bring them to mother's that afternoon.

I was glad to have them safe with her and not mussed or soiled. I was so proud of them; every stitch had been put in by hand, involving months of sewing with the daintiest of embroideries and the finest of lawn.

As I packed my handbag, by good luck I picked up all my toilet articles including my toothbrush, which was more than my poor husband did, much to his discomfort in the following weeks. His beautiful clothes were still stacked in the corner ready to be carried away, so we couldn't leave those. And we had another inconceivable burden — a sewing machine! As I was planning a new outfit after my baby's arrival, I had brought my little Wilcox and Gibbs with its hand attachment, intending later on to "have in" the sewing woman with patterns and style books.

The machine was heavy, but my mother insisted we could carry it. The sewing machine must go! So, with two suitcases, Hugh's two stacked suitboxes, and a sewing machine, we stepped out of the Palace Hotel onto Market Street.

Massive confusion met our eyes. We walked slowly up the streets, past the White House department store, where thousands of dollars worth of real lace fluttered softly in the morning breeze through shattered show windows. We climbed the hill to the Colonial Hotel, where my grandmother lived, and there I stayed until late in the afternoon, while Hugh and Mother, laden with our luggage, continued up the Powell Street hill to our home.

At the time we separated in the morning, none of us had any idea of the magnitude of the disaster that had overtaken San Francisco. We knew the earthquake had been more severe than any we had ever had before; but we didn't realize that the water mains had been severed, and that our fire chief had been killed in his bed by falling brick. We knew only later, when information spread from one frightened citizen to another. What was ahead of us?

Through the rest of the day my grandmother and I sat at the window, watching the horse-drawn trucks from business houses carrying goods to the outskirts of the city for safekeeping. Large trucks from Shreve's and Gump's department stores raced up and down, loaded with massive silver trays, candelabra, pictures, and objects of art, every priceless object unwrapped and exposed to the soft rain of cinders. Two men with shotguns rode on each truck.

About four o'clock we started the long walk up and over the Powell Street hill to my mother's home. Laboriously I lifted my heavy body up the steep grade. Although I was empty-handed, by this time I was plainly feeling the exhaustion of shock, but my pioneer grandmother, who fifty years before had walked the Isthmus with a baby in her arms, took it in stride without a word of complaint. How I wished later I had taken an armful from my grandmother's room — ornaments, jewelry, lace. Everything was burned, but at that time we did not dream the fire would reach so far.

We stopped on the crest of Nob Hill to look at the blazing sheets of flame and smoke stretching for blocks in two different parts of the city: one wall of fire was in the wholesale district to the east, the other in the south far out Market Street, with, in between, a smaller blaze which had started near the Grand Opera House. Those two great curtains of flame would ultimately join the smaller center fire, creating a conflagration that would sweep everything before it.

Dr. Tevis, across the street from our home, had opened his palatial residence to some of the members of the opera company, and from time to time we saw Plancon and Gadski and Melba watching the activity from the veranda. All day long Dr. Tevis' liveried coachman walked his team of horses, hitched to a Victoria, back and forth in front of the house, prepared to move the distinguished guests farther if the fire should threaten.

By six in the evening, our immediate family had assembled at my parents' home. All gas in the city had been shut off, and every chimney had been shaken down. By order of the police, fires of any kind, whether for cooking or for lighting, were forbidden inside buildings. My father, good camper that he was, prepared a wonderful dinner. An excavation in the next block furnished material for the campfire, and Father broiled steaks bought in the neighborhood, heated canned corn, and made coffee. It was the first food any of us had had that day, and we sat on the curb eating heartily. This might be the last meal we would have for some time.

All through the evening we sat on the front porch, watching the crowds surging up over the hill. We could see them plainly by the light from the fire in the city — a sickly yellow flush in the foreground, turning into a red glow in the distance. The crowds were very still: no talk, no banter, no quarreling.

At last, about two o'clock, it was decided that I would be safer at the home of Nellie Mason, a lifelong friend of my mother, who lived at the edge of the Presidio. Hugh found an exhausted horse and a cab, and we three women started the seven-mile drive toward the Presidio, carrying the same luggage we had brought from the Palace, together with some treasures of my mother's. She tied them in sheets and piled the cab high with these laundry-looking bundles. My father and Hugh stayed behind. It was each person's determination to stay with his property until ordered away by the soldiers. When Mary Belle had left after dinner, Mother told her we would go to Nellie Mason's, but we were all sure the fire would be controlled long before it reached the hilltops.

We arrived at Mrs. Mason's home about four o'clock in the morning. She wasn't too pleased to see us; already about twenty of her relatives and friends were there, but she offered us such hospitality as she had.

Mother and I were put in one of the servants' rooms on the third floor; the maids, as well as my grandmother, were downstairs on sofas. It was only fitful sleeping any of us could do, since at any moment another heavy shake could send us into the street. But at least we had shelter. My own small world was concerned only with my personal well-being. My child was evidently feeling the effect of the shock and lay still in my body for long periods of time, then trembled with a spasm far too violent and relapsed again into hours of quiet.

Late in the afternoon Mary Belle arrived to tell us that she had been ordered away from her home. She was intending to go to San Anselmo, across the Golden Gate in Marin County, to stay with friends. She would walk through the Presidio to the beach, from where, she had heard, people were being taken out to the ferries in small boats manned by soldiers, thence across to Marin County, where the interurban trains were still running. Then she told me that she had had to leave all my baby clothes except the prettiest dress.

Now my precious baby clothes were gone! I told myself she had left her home carrying all she could stagger under; it was only fair that my things should be left behind; but I went off into the conservatory alone and shed some tears. I was overcome by the first realization of personal loss. When my husband and my father arrived about evening, Hugh found me still grieving alone and told me how silly I was. But I grieved silently all through the succeeding weeks. The most beautiful layettes from the finest New York stores would never make up for the loss of the things I had made myself.

Naturally, Hugh was determined to get word to his family in Ohio, and he was eager to communicate with his office in Tonopah. He left me early the next morning to try to reach a telegraph office across the bay in Oakland, with the understanding he would be back by nightfall.

Too many have described the days after the earthquake, days filled with comedy, pathos, tragedy. The most tragic people I saw were the tiny-footed Chinese women who walked all the miles over our terrible hills on their tortured, deformed feet, bound in childhood according to custom. Out there by the Presidio, they inched themselves along by anything to which they could cling, winding their fingers into fences, leaning on low copings. The memory of their pain-wracked faces stays with me, together with the scuffing sound of trunks and beds and wagons and skates, anything that could be made to do duty as a carrier.

As the third night settled down, Hugh had not returned. Reports came of men impressed into service down in the fire region, of men collapsing with the strain and being carried off, unknown, to emergency hospitals. All that night I sat on the edge of the coping around our friend's garden, watching.

Unknown to me, my poor husband was having his own share of trouble. When Hugh walked onto the Oakland ferry, no one told him he couldn't get back into San Francisco. The city was under martial law; the soldiers were instructed to keep every possible person out of the city area. After several days, with the help of an official of the Southern Pacific Railroad, he was able to get back into San Francisco. Hugh walked all night. In the pink-tinted darkness of the morning, we met in the center of the street and cried in each other's arms. Hugh was completely done in; he lay on the couch in one of the rooms and slept twelve hours with all the noise and the people constantly walking through the room.

One good thing that came out of this trip was that down in the burned area, engaged in relief work, Hugh met the minister who had married us. This gentleman told Hugh to stay where we were, and as soon as he could secure a proper conveyance, he would come for us and take us out of the city.

Day by day food and water became more scarce. Besides this, we were all getting awfully dirty. Water was brought into the city in watering carts, and my father and Mrs. Mason's Chinese cook went to the place in our district where it was available, but it was many blocks away and not much could be carried at a time. On one of these trips my father met a bakery wagon distributing loaves of bread. It was stale but edible, and we were glad to eat it dry.

Sometime in the following week, our minister arrived with an express wagon and an old mattress rolled up. On this grandmother and I sat, while Hugh and my mother and father sat on the rear of the wagon, their feet dangling over the back. We still had with us the sewing machine, the boxes of Hugh's clothes and mother's bundles of "laundry."

As we approached the burned area, the devastation that met our eyes was fantastic. North, east, and south, we saw nothing but miles and miles of smoking ruins and drifting ash. The progress of the fire had been checked only a few days earlier, but already the streets were being cleared so that some sort of regular life could be resumed. Our bundle around us, we crossed San Francisco Bay on the ferry and huddled into the local train for Alameda, where we were met by Hugh's brother Masons. We were taken to the Shrine Temple, where we washed in heavenly warm water, and were given food: roast beef, potatoes, even hot biscuits and coffee! The next day Hugh advertised in the local paper for a furnished flat, and soon we were comfortably settled. Here we stayed until our son was born, a few weeks later.

As soon as transportation in the Bay Area was possible, my father started out to locate my sister in San Anselmo. Except for the fatigue, she and her little child had not suffered. In the course of my father's talk with her, he said: "Poor little Marjorie is grieving over the loss of her baby clothes." Mary Belle answered him in some amazement, "Why, I have all her baby clothes." Then my sister remembered, she had forgotten we knew nothing of what happened to her after she left us at Nellie Mason's home. Instead of going straight through the Presidio and out of the city, she had decided to return once more to her home, and on the way back she stumbled across a child's wagon. She grabbed it and ran. Before the soldiers could order her away from the danger zone again, she gathered a few things she had regretfully left behind and walked across the Presidio, dragging the loaded wagon behind her. So, to my intense and tearful joy, my father returned with my layette, crumpled and soiled, to be sure, but intact.

As for the sewing machine, it had been a bone of contention at every move we made, but nothing we could do or say would persuade my mother to abandon it. When at last we reached the haven of Alameda, she went out to buy clothes for us, but the stores were completely sold out. Triumphantly, she came back with a bolt of muslin, some trimming and spools of white thread. Hour after hour she sat at that sewing machine, grinding away on its handmotor, and by the end of another week, each of us had a change of nightgown and chemise. The whole set of her body said, "I told you so."

And what of Hugh and the new wardrobe he had purchased the day before the earthquake? After I arrived in Alameda, I wore my mother's coat while my one dress was being cleaned, and it came back looking more bedraggled than ever. But Hugh! Inside twenty-four hours he blossomed out in a light grey suit, new shirt, new socks, new hankie. And me? Still in my awful maternity dress and incongruous black lace hat (with plumes, remember?).

After our son was born, Hugh returned to Tonopah. I finally acquired the promised new outfit and then, with tiny Hugh and the completely restored layette, I too took the train for Nevada.

FROM THE TIME OF ITS DISCOVERY, Tonopah had been financed by eastern investors, but as the new camps came along, California speculators became more and more actively involved. As a result of the earthquake, development money from California, previously so easy to secure, dried up almost overnight. This situation became part of a chain reaction extending across the nation in 1907, and the financial panic began. One morning in October the three Tonopah banks failed to open.

The news came to me by telephone. I had no real comprehension of what the bank closings would mean to Tonopah or to us personally, but instinctively I knew we were faced with misfortune. From my windows I could see groups of men on every street corner, talking excitedly. I asked Fong to watch out for little Hugh and skipped down the hill to Jen Stock's house. I had to talk to someone, and she was so levelheaded. But she wasn't home, so I continued on over the hill to see Pearl Bartlett.

George and Pearl Bartlett had just moved into a really magnificent home. It was rumored to have cost $75,000. I think I had expected to find her in tears, but to my astonishment Pearl met me with a bright smile.

"Hello," she said. "What does all this mean to you and Hugh?" She spoke as if it were a new strike instead of a calamity.

"I don't know," I replied; "like everybody else, we've invested a lot of money, but I know Hugh's pretty cautious. He'd never be tempted to go in too deeply."

Pearl threw back her head and laughed. "We'll be skinned alive." Then she added quickly, "But it was wonderful while it lasted. You know, Marjorie, they can't take away from us what we've already had."

I never forgot that remark. I never forgot her gay laugh either, although we both knew the family would be bound with chains of debt for years. In a few months the Bartletts were living in a rented cottage in Reno, stripped of all they owned, but as happy on the surface as they were when stocks were soaring.

Most of our friends were involved in the collapse in one way or another, and they all seemed to take it lightly. The gambler's code is not to squeal when he loses. But my own reactions were deep and slow. I knew Hugh's clients — the Mine Operators' Association, the Tonopah and Goldfield Railroad, and one of the banks — would continue to pay him handsomely for his advice, but what of those shares of stock in mines all over southern Nevada that had made us so rich on paper? We had had holdings worth close to a million dollars, and their value was rising with every market day. Now most of them were worthless, or had been put up as security on ventures that were lost. Hugh uttered no word of regret, but for me a dream of great wealth had suddenly been shattered.

I made no brief for myself — the dramatic temperament is a law unto itself. It is as futile to ask it to be calm in storm as to expect it not to be gay when skies are fair. Life in Tonopah had meant romance and excitement; present hardship had been the prelude to future luxury. Now my depression was so deep that not even the birth of our second son in May, 1908, could lift me out of it. Whipped by the dead dream, I told myself I wasn't meant to be domestic, that I had need of self-expression my youth had promised.

The magic had gone out of living. I looked at that open country with different eyes. By 1910, all I could see were the unpainted shacks in the foreground, the dusty, winding paths that were the streets, the never-ending monotony. What did it matter to me that distant colors were beautiful, that sunset reddened into gold? What did it matter to me that people were loyal and lovable, that little children needed care? That woman in Hawthorne, was this what she saw ahead of me? Disappointment? Disillusionment, magnified and intensified by desert limitations?

That first day when Jen Stock came to call, she had said, "I did not want you to be lonely. I wanted you to know you had neighbors."

And Bessie Barndt, at Hot Creek Ranch, had said things to me that at the time I thought a bit melodramatic. "Don't talk to me about the desert," she whispered, her voice trembling with emotion, "that vast stretch of open country you're raving about. That desert is alive, and it'll fight you. The stillness?" Her voice was rising as she spoke. "I've started down at the corral, and I've run to the house and slammed the door on it as if it were an animal creeping up on me, ready to tear me to pieces. Don't talk to me about the stillness of the desert in those high-faluting words. *You don't know what you're talking about!*"

And Sadie Bell, at beautiful Reese River, with her embroidered dish towels and sheets. I remember saying to her with all the arrogance of youth, "Sadie, how can you do such needless handwork? Those embroidered dish towels are red with the blood of murdered time!" Quietly she answered, "When the men ride the roundup, I'm alone. Sometimes they are gone for three months. What else can I do but embroider things that *can* be embroidered to keep from going crazy?"

I lived all my desert years in a town where I had no water to haul, no washing to be hung out in the blistering sun, no livestock to care for in the bitter wind. But that desert crept into my thoughts until it looked, not like an open plain, but like a pit closing me in, with sides stretching to the sky. There was nothing beyond the dump on the edge of town, nothing but the stark realism of the foreground, and myself.

I took refuge in reading, anything to keep me from thinking. The Harvard Classics were at hand, but most of what I read was just soporific. At last I got around to Shakespeare, and here Hugh's fine collection of Shakespeare served me even better than it had served Herman Knickerbocker. Finally, beyond this lonely effort to make peace with myself came a new experience.

It was dear Sadie Bell who set in motion the train of events that proved my salvation. She was a daughter-in-law of Senator T. J. Bell, at whose ranch we had visited. Some of the Bells were always coming into town on holidays, and one day Sadie took a jaunt up the hill to visit me. In the course of conversation, she asked me how I'd like to come to the ranch for the spring roundup. I was surprised by the invitation, for in that day ranch women never rode with the men. It just wasn't done. Although I was listless about everything, this was something I really wanted to do, and I accepted with alacrity.

The trip by autostage brought me to the ranch in the late afternoon. When my baggage had been deposited in the large, high-ceilinged bedroom, I put on my riding togs, and Elmer Bell, Sadie's older brother-in-law, took me down to the corral. He pointed out a cowpony, old and wise, which, he told me, knew as much about rounding up cattle as the men did. He would take good care of me.

At dinner I was introduced to two cattle buyers who had come in to look over the herd and to the men on the ranch, most of whom would ride with me the next day. One, "Bud," a tall blond cowboy about thirty, had class even in blue jeans. I perked up when Mr. Bell assigned him to ride with me.

At five o'clock the next morning, the bell rang down at the bunkhouse, and by five-thirty everybody was at breakfast. Sadie presided over the big stove, with the help of the old hired man who was part of the equipment of every ranch. What a breakfast we had! Home-cured bacon and ham, baking-powder biscuits, hot cakes, blackberry jam, and currant jelly made from the wild berries that grew in profusion behind the ranch house. By six o'clock we were down at the corral, with a private rodeo and a thrill a minute until everyone was safely mounted.

In the cold morning air the horses were all fractious, and for a few minutes it looked as if excitement would be changed into tragedy. As a cowboy mounted, one of the cattle buyers tossed a saddle blanket on the ground in front of the horse. The startled pony reared and then plunged toward the fence with the evident intention of scraping off its rider. But the boy kept his head and managed to bring the frightened animal under control. Corral practical jokes are often pretty rough.

Bud was a professional horsebreaker, and it was up to him to ride the bad ones. This first morning his horse stood crouched back on his haunches, ears flat, nostrils flaring. Slowly Bud walked up to him, rested his hand gently on the horse's neck, whispering softly and then leaped lightly into the saddle. The rebellious animal bucked a few times and then settled down. Unlike most of the other riders, Bud wore no spurs. When I remarked on this to Sadie, she said he never wore them; it was his pride to control a horse only by his gentle voice and firm hand on the reins.

I was introduced to the others—two men from each of the surrounding ranches whose livestock roamed this range. The custom is to round up the cattle from all the ranches; then on the last day each team parts out its own herd to drive away to the home ranch.

At the head of the contingent from the Bell ranch was Elmer Bell, overseer of his father's vast acreage, a big heavy man with round but handsome features and fine eyes. He was a superb horseman, Sadie told me, who could ride a horse all day over rough country and bring it home fresh, when other men, lighter but without his finesse, would ride the animal to exhaustion over the same terrain. Another family member was Sam Worthington, a tall, lean Kentuckian, who sat his saddle with no style at all and wore jeans and a dirty black hat. This is not an attractive description, perhaps, and yet "Mr. Sam" had a very real charm. He had come to the Bell ranch as a young cowboy, had married one of the Bell daughters, and was now boss of his wife's miles of grazing land. He knew every animal individually, and when it came to parting out cattle, Bud said Mr. Sam was a genius.

When all were mounted, we rode a couple of miles down the road, where we stopped at the point from which the cowboys would scatter out over the hills, two by two, to round up the cattle. We would search for them in the surrounding canyons and then drive them to an appointed central spot. Because we were riding the Bell range that day, Elmer Bell was the master of the range and designated the direction each pair of riders should take. Etiquette of the cattle country makes it incumbent upon the master to assume the longest, hardest ride himself.

Tomorrow we would ride to a different point of the compass, and some other member of the party would be the master of the range.

Of course, as the tenderfoot, I was given the shortest ride to the appointed roundup site. As the men spread out, or "sprangled" as it was called, Bud and I started straight ahead and loafed along for hours, gathering in any cow and her calf we saw. The babies had been born since the cows had been turned out in the fall, and the cute little white-faced creatures showed their astonishment and concern at the appearance of this strange beast, a man on a horse, something unmistakably new to their experience. Blatting a rhythmic *"bah-ah-ah-ah"* in time with their own hoofbeats, they tagged along beside their blasé mothers.

Arriving at the roundup spot long before anyone else, Bud and I sat our horses and took in the scene, new and delightful to me, although old-hat to Bud. Soon in the distance, too far away to be anything but a drifting blur, little trickles of a moving brown mass began to appear over every hilltop. Like blobs of molasses, the huddled cattle trickled down the sides of the hills to combine into larger streams, all flowing toward the roundup spot. Looking like sprites, the cowboys dashed around, the faint coyote-like *"yip"* of the men blending at last with the bawling of the cattle as the mass resolved itself into individual animals. By midafternoon we were all met, sitting our horses in a huge ring, heads toward center to keep the cattle inside. Every so often some unresigned steer bolted the herd; the nearest cowboy dashed after him, lariat swinging and horse agallop, to bring the creature to a sudden halt, jolted head over heels by the rope on neck or foot.

I was sorry for the poor beasts taking that terrible jolt at full tilt, and said so. One of the boys looked over at me and answered sympathetically, "You're telling me?"

Bud laughed. "He played football in high school. He knows how it feels."

About four o'clock, strung out in a wide backline, we began the trek home, driving the cattle ahead of us, seven hundred, eight hundred, maybe more. By sundown we rode into the lower corral, then trudged slowly back to the ranch house across the meadow.

Oh, how every bone and muscle in my body ached! At the end of that first day I was crippled. On the second day I thought the only thing to do was to die. I was so done in that my friends were concerned, but by the morning of the third I had recovered, and from then on the tensions within me began to loosen.

Every day brought some new experience — for instance, two bull-fights. As the cattle came down the hillside to join the mass, there was a sudden disturbance in parts of the herd. The bulls had caught the odor of one another! The cows milled around as the bulls began to paw the ground. Throwing great clouds of dust over their backs, they moved slowly but inexorably through the tightly packed mass of animals with low, ominous rumbling. When they met, the rest of the cattle jumped out of the path of the monsters. They dashed at each other with the ponderous speed of two railroad engines, heads lowered, sharp horns ready for attack. Back and forth they pushed one another, each trying to get his horns into the neck or shoulder of the other. Finally a smear of blood appeared on the side of one bull and spread darkly through his thick hair. Back and forth they surged, perhaps for an hour. The power and beauty of the spectacle was thrilling.

"Don't get too close," warned Bud. "Pretty soon one of them guys is goin' to decide he's had enough, and he'll bolt. He's blind as a bat and won't look where he's goin'. You better not be in the way." All the way back to the ranch, one old warrior coughed and coughed. He had a big gash in his side and hung his dusty, powerful head. His cows milled around their warrior with eyes tense and tails stiff, licking his eyes, his nose, his sides, showing every evidence of deep concern.

I learned so much during that week. Bud told me of the subterfuge a cow can use to make the coyote overlook her baby hidden in the thicket; about the wonderful law of nature that sends a calf lost from its mother back to the spot where it last suckled. I felt great sympathy for the cows that kept dashing out of the herd to search for calves left behind, and was always grateful when the men let them go.

The dogies, those pathetic little babies that had lost their mothers, were so thin that their little bones almost stuck through their hides, and their legs wobbled crazily under their slight weight. It became our job, Bud's and mine, to drive the dogies home. We would arrive sometimes an hour after the others, with the weak, slow-moving little things. Very often Bud or I would carry one across the saddle.

As we were jogging along one day, we heard Mr. Sam's voice calling faintly from a great distance, "Bu-u-d, cattle in the mahawganees." Bud dashed up the hill and disappeared among the scrub mahogany trees. My horse was determined to follow. It was all I could do to keep from being decapitated by the low branches. Then about a dozen steers appeared and raced down toward a swift stream on the floor of the canyon, and again my horse was determined to follow, but I was not! Bud appeared from among the trees and called to me, "Did you see the cattle?" It was nothing to him or my horse that I had nearly lost my head.

I yelled at the top of my voice, "They went down into the creek bed!" Bud plunged down the hillside. I did not follow him and felt like a quitter, but I knew that that narrow canyon with the rushing stream was no place for a tenderfoot. I heard him sloshing about and shouting among the willows. Finally he climbed out of the canyon, driving the steers in front of him. He started them down the opposite side of the hill and then turned his attention to his horse.

Two men could have turned those cattle with ease, but he had had to use his horse so hard that she was breathing heavily, and her legs were scratched by the jagged rocks. Feeling inadequate, I watched him as he unsaddled her and looked around for a proper piece of wood to curry her with. Then he took off his bandana and wiped her eyes and muzzle. If he had been a woman with a hurt child, he could not have been more tender.

No matter what walk of life a man may fill, there is always a certain flair, an unmistakable air of competence that constitutes aristocracy, whether he is a financial genius, a wizard engineer, or a professional wrangler. The way Bud sat his horse, the way his kerchief flowed over his shoulder, the angle at which he held his reins — all marked him as a member of that breed.

The last day of the roundup, I rode with Sam Worthington. We would be going higher up on the mountains than I had ever been before. Mr. Sam and I circled slowly around the hills, jogging on and on, hour after hour. At last we started to climb the mountain to go over the ridge. Once we passed through a band of sheep. Mr. Sam, with a cattleman's hatred of the creatures, never even looked at them. But I looked back and yelled, "Look, Mr. Sam. Look at the sheep in the sagebrush. They look like maggots in green cheese." He kept on climbing.

Suddenly we topped the ridge, and I halted to gaze breathlessly at the view before me. Ranges of mountains, towering one over another, marched away into the distance until the last was only a grey-blue film. Hundreds of feet below us lay the central spot of the roundup, with the familiar brown mass in the center and the distance between filled with curved lines of mountain and plain for miles and miles in every direction. The effect on me was staggering. I thought of every significant line of outdoor poetry I had ever encountered. The one that echoed in my memory now with realization, was Henry Van Dyke's line from "God of the Open Air":

Oh, how the sight of the things
that are great enlarges the eyes!

The vastness, the eternal quiet, the beingness! Here again no green appeared except the dull grey-green of the sage in the foreground, but tan and brown and lavender, pink and those wonderful pastel blues that shade off into grey. Something within me was released. Tears flooded my eyes. I felt as if all the littlenesses clinging to my character could be swept away if I could capture the bigness of that moment. I had a revelation of the significance of life, something to be grasped no matter how tragic the details of living might become. I wanted to throw up my arms and shout, "Yippee!" as the boys did.

Then, driving the cattle ahead of us, we slowly descended into the afternoon shadows and finally joined the other cowboys on the plain.

That night at dinner Mr. Sam said, "Mrs. Brown's got a new name for the sheep. She calls 'em maggots!" He spit out the word, and everybody laughed. But my remark had hit a bullseye, and from then on I knew I belonged.

The last days were used to part out. Two men started into the herd, spotted a cow, nosed her and her calf toward the edge of the group, and with a sudden "swish" flipped her out of the mass and sent her off to join the rest of the cattle bearing the same brand. Here's where Sam Worthington's genius showed up. When evening of the last day came, each team started away down the lane with its own herd. The spring roundup was over.

The next day I took the stage home. In parting I hugged Sadie with tearful gratitude for this wonderful experience. She didn't know it, but I knew I had reached the turning point. The encircling desert would never again close in upon me and trap my spirit in despair.

FROM TIME TO TIME since we had been married, Hugh had talked about having a bookplate made. After my return from Reese River, we agreed that this was the time to do it. Together we worked out a design consisting of sagebrush in the foreground, with a road winding off into high mountains. Across the top of the little sketch Hugh drew a line of books and wrote LAW at one end and ROMANCE at the other. Above the books in his fine hand-lettering, he printed a new motto: AS WE JOURNEY THROUGH LIFE LET US LIVE BY THE WAY.

Whether Hugh had connived with Sadie Bell to give me the unique experience of riding the roundup, I never knew. At any rate, he was elated by the effect the trip had upon me. The contact with the out-of-doors for so many days, the hard riding, the skilled precision and teamwork of the men, the new connotations in living opened my eyes to my own stilted system of values. Putting the motto to work, as it were, I made a silent and solemn vow to make the least of all that was gone and the most of today.

Tonopah had been affected by the general depression, of course, but our town did not experience the "boom-and-bust" that had been the pattern of so many mining camps. The state as a whole was prosperous because of Nevada's amazing variety of minerals. We were never quite so gay again, and the colorful characters who had come to Tonopah for the quick money were siphoned off through Goldfield, but the solid citizens — the geologists, the chemists, the mine superintendents and their wives, as well as many merchants and busines men — made up the strong base for our community.

We were no longer exciting enough to attract top theatrical stars, as we had been a few years earlier when stars like Grace George came to us direct from New York, and the popular young actress Clara Kimball Young visited us and displayed her fantastic collection of jewels. But we did have the opportunity to entertain Constance Crawley, a lively British actress on her first visit to the United States. With her leading man and her manager, she came to luncheon on the Sunday they arrived to prepare for the Monday night performance. That same Sunday, in the big sprawling sports arena that had just been erected in the lower end of town, the young Jack Dempsey was barnstorming, fighting for fifty cents a round, we were told.

Miss Crawley went on to San Francisco to fill an engagement there, and was interviewed by one of the papers about her experiences in the Wild West. The article said she had attended the fights, but of course that was not true. The time had not yet arrived when women went to prizefights. She sat with us on the porch listening to the distant roars of the crowd at the arena.

Miss Crawley was a thoroughly delightful person, very British and genuinely interested in the mining camp. Alas, we were not able to stage any such show as had been trumped up for Elinor Glyn in Goldfield a few years earlier. Maybe we should have let Miss Crawley go to the fights.

Incidentally, Miss Crawley inadvertently furnished the title for this book. When she arrived in San Francisco, she was quoted as saying, "There is a lady in Tonopah, Mrs. Hugh Brown . . ." My friends had a lot to say about that!

Another visitor whom I recall with particular delight was Ralph Waldo Trine, who wrote *In Tune with the Infinite*. He was a popular philosopher of the day.

There was a severe drought in Nevada that year, and from all over the state cattle were being sent to the rich pasture lands of California. One day I heard that a herd from the Barndt ranch at Hot Creek was to be shipped from our railroad station. I thought a glimpse of authentic western life would interest this gentleman from the East, so I took Mr. Trine in our Thomas Flyer to the emergency corrals erected on the edge of town. The men and cattle were exhausted, for they had traveled many slow miles to reach the railroad. As we approached the dusty, noisy scene, where tired cowboys prodded weakened cattle into the cattle runs and then pushed them into the boxcars, I saw a cowboy I had met on one of my visits to Bessie Barndt.

I called him over. "I want to introduce you to Mr. Trine," I said.

The cowboy paused, then asked "Did you say *Trine?*"

"That's right."

"Oh," he drawled, "there's a writer by that name."

"Yes," I answered. "This is Ralph Waldo Trine, who wrote *In Tune with the Infinite.*"

The cowboy shook his head. At last he said slowly, "My wife and I read your book. We think it's about the best book we ever read. I never expected I'd be meeting you." Mr. Trine beamed, and extended his hand. Here was a man who wrote philosophy face to face with a cowhand right off the range who knew and treasured his book. It was one of those rare moments of fulfillment that must be so precious to an author.

As our aspirations for wealth tapered off, so our personal horizons expanded. Hugh's activities in the interests of the legal profession began to extend over the entire state, and then onto the national scene as well.

His connection with the American Bar Association had begun with his law school days. When he attended the sessions in 1907 and 1908, Hugh was shocked to hear the outspoken condemnation of Nevada for its easy divorce laws. After the legislature shortened the residential requirements, the class of lawyers flooding the state and the kind of law they practiced were most objectionable. Knowing the high caliber of the state's resident lawyers, the disapproval troubled him seriously, and he spent a large part of the year 1909 bringing to the attention of the reputable lawyers of the state the immediate necessity of creating a strong legal organization to curb the flagrant abuses. Through his determination, the Nevada State Bar Association was chartered in 1910. In recognition of his efforts, Hugh was elected its first president.

Our little boys were still too young for me to leave them and accompany Hugh on his trips east to meetings of the American Bar Association, of which he had been a member since law school days. But I did go with him when business took him to nearby places. One such occasion arose when a serious water litigation case came up in Lovelock. Hugh's client was Mrs. Arthur Rogers, a wealthy widow from San Francisco, who owned hundreds of acres of ranchland in Pershing County.

Mrs. Rogers was a Lady Bountiful. During our stay in Lovelock, she had all kinds of delicacies shipped in daily from San Francisco, even flowers in huge boxes. These lovely blossoms were distributed throughout the lobby and the dining room of the hotel, as well as in the rooms we occupied.

The day the trial ended, Mrs. Rogers gave us one of these great boxes from the florist. Arriving home in Tonopah, I telephoned to a few friends to come in to tea. I planned that when the front door was opened, all the flowers would be on display. To accomplish this taxed every utensil I owned.

In the afternoon when my friends arrived, they could hardly credit their eyes. Never had any of us seen so much color in Tonopah. Even when we had a wet year and the pale desert flowers of Nevada burst into bloom, there was hardly more than a faint glow of color; but here was a profusion of yellow roses, deep pink peonies, purple iris, daffodils, delphiniums, and carnations. After tea, I told each lady to help herself to the blossoms she most desired. I wanted them to feel that they had gathered their own bouquets. When Mrs. Rogers offered me that box of flowers, she gave us all a beautiful experience.

During these years the national resources of lumber, minerals, and water were being concentrated in private ownership. As an associated evil, tariffs and freight rates were progressively more unjust to the middle and western states. In 1911 voices in the West were accusing "vested interests" of forming legislative committees composed of railroad henchmen or campaign contributors for the purpose of passing laws to control these tariffs. Besides the demand for a referendum by means of which partisan or crippling laws could be repealed by popular vote, the public clamor began to demand the recall of judges who were accused of interpreting the laws to the advantage of powerful interests.

Hugh sympathized with pleas for justice to the West, but he was alarmed by the danger to the judicial system inherent in any move to recall judges by popular vote. In 1912, when he was invited to make the commencement address at the University of Nevada, my husband took the opportunity to express his opinions on this grave matter.

The following year I accompanied Hugh when he went to the American Bar Association meeting in Milwaukee. At the opening session a gentleman rose to make an announcement from the floor. Hugh whispered to me that he was chairman of the Committee on the Recall. When he began to speak, I glanced at Hugh with indrawn breath, for, holding a small pamphlet above his head, he said: "Mr. Chairman, I wish to call to the attention of the Association this address given by Mr. Hugh Brown of Nevada on the dangers of the recall of judges. It is the most competent and comprehensive treatment of the subject that has come to my attention." After this commendation, Hugh was interviewed that day by many lawyers. During the session he was appointed to the Committee on the Recall, and membership on other important committees followed rapidly.

14: ♦ ♦

As THE WONDERFUL AND BUSY YEARS ADVANCED, the early comers who had struck it rich in Nevada mining became established citizens and men of power in the state. Many, like Hugh, moved onto a larger stage.

Tasker Oddie, long the "first citizen" of Tonopah, was inevitably one of these. With the passing years, Tasker had played in unbelievably bad luck. All over the state he poured money into mining ventures without success. At last he was back to the impecunious state of his early manhood, and his beloved ranch in Monitor Valley was turned over to one of the banks.

In 1911, Tasker decided to run for the governorship. He had all the requisites for political success except one — money. But he refused to let that stop him. With his last few dollars he overhauled his old Thomas Flyer and started across the desert to the nearest town.

Without cash Tasker could not rent halls, but he could meet the people on the streets with the same hearty handshake he had used when he was rich. He had to sleep in hotels when no friend offered him a bed; but often next morning the hotelman, like as not a one-time partner, would wish him Godspeed with a wave of the hand. Even his posters appeared miraculously ahead of him. Tasker accepted it all with his genial, affectionate smile.

On election night, after Tasker had won, he and Hugh sat in a cafe in Reno. Tasker pulled out of his pocket a picture postcard of the governor's mansion in Carson City — a handsome, yellow, porticoed building with white pillars, set in the center of a dignified garden. "Look, Hugh," he said. "There's my new home." Then, with that infectious Oddie chuckle, he added, "It was either that or a tent."

When the time came for Tasker's inauguration, Hugh and I went to Carson to stand in his receiving line. The hall where the reception was held was one of those awful rooms that had survived from the Comstock days, with dark wood paneling extending half way up the wall and gold medallion wallpaper above. This night the ugliness had been masked by floating bunting and draped chandeliers until the place took on the festive atmosphere that surrounded Tasker's election all over the state.

When the new governor made his entrance, for a moment the crowd was still. Tears flooded many eyes. In the center of the immense room Tasker stopped and gripped the hand of the nearest guest, his face flushed and his bald head crimson with happy embarrassment. Ranchers, ample and affluent; cattlemen, lean and sunburned; miners and cowboys and businessmen; all the types that represent "Nevada" pressed forward to shake the hand of the governor.

For me the launching of the battleship that bore our state's name was the high point of Governor Oddie's term of office. Hugh and I were invited to attend this event as members of the governor's party on July 11, 1914.

The day we rolled into Boston, we were escorted to the Copley Plaza Hotel. The room reserved for us was much finer than anything we had ever seen before, spacious and high-ceilinged. In a few moments there was a knock at the door, and a neat little maid entered. She informed me she had been assigned to me for the time of my residence at the hotel. I was staggered! I thanked her and said I was unaccustomed to a maid, and my simple wardrobe could not make use of her services. And she departed.

For three days we were dined and wined like royalty. Many celebrities were present, among them Josephus Daniels, then Secretary of the Navy, and a tall blond young man, with very upright carriage and a flashing smile. He was a real personality — the young Assistant Secretary of the Navy, Franklin Delano Roosevelt.

On the day of the launching, we were breakfast guests of Charles Schwab, president of the Bethlehem Steel Company. During the meal Mr. Schwab asked for ideas for a present for the little sponsor, Tasker's twelve-year-old niece Eleanor Siebert. I called across the table suggesting a wristwatch. After breakfast, at Mr. Schwab's request, I accompanied him down into the business district of Boston to one of the fashionable jewelry stores.

There we examined several exquisite watches and selected one of blue enamel, the face of which was surrounded by a circle of diamonds. In its velvet case, the gift was entrusted to my care until the time of presentation. No one who bore any responsibility toward the launching of that great battleship felt more important than I.

Speaking of the launching reminds me that it was here I made the prize "boner" of my life. As we all stood on the platform waiting for the great dreadnaught to slip majestically off the ways, I turned to the young man at my side and said, laughingly, "Suppose she sticks?" A look of genuine pain came into his face, as if he had been stabbed with a knife. He muttered something in a strangled voice. I was appalled at his reaction, and much more so when I learned afterward that he was the engineer directly responsible for placing the stulls (the timbers) that held the ship rigid on the ways. If she stuck, he would be to blame. Days before the event the fear of such a catastrophe grows progressively greater. The engineer can't sleep or eat. He is overcome with nausea. In my ignorance, I had said the unforgivable words to the one man to whom they should never have been said.

Eleanor crashed the bottle of champagne against her prow and shouted, "I christen you *Nevada!*" The great ship flung aside the last few logs that held her firm; they sounded like pistol shots as they sprang away. Smoke from the friction rose like a veil behind her as she dropped gracefully off the ways into the water.

At that time the *Nevada* was considered the last word in naval architecture. When Hugh and I went aboard, I was not up to appreciating the caliber of the guns and the set of the turrets, but we were both thrilled by the magnificence of the silver service made from five thousand ounces of silver donated by the miners of Tonopah. The coffee urns, the trays, the candelabra, the punchbowl and cups were heavy and ornate, made from original designs illustrating events in the history of the state. They are now on exhibition in the Smithsonian Institution in Washington, D.C.*

Key Pittman, a marked contrast to Tasker Oddie, was elected to the United States Senate in 1913, where he served until his death in 1940. As senator from the leading silver-producing state, he was for many years head of the "silver bloc," consisting of senators from all the silver-producing states. Mrs. Pittman was a very successful hostess during her many years in Washington. Like her husband, she had glamour. No woman could make a trip down the Yukon Trail alone without some of the glitter of the adventure rubbing off on her.

A politician as cold-blooded as a gunman, Key was often bitterly attacked. His enemies maintained that the United States silver program sponsored by him had contributed to China's ruin, and the repercussions of it would be felt for generations by the entire world. Even Key's friends accused him of being ungrateful, while his foes called him ruth-

---

*The *Nevada* was used as a target ship when the first atomic bomb was exploded at the Bikini Atoll in 1946. Although she received the full fury of the blast, it did not sink her. Ultimately, she was scuttled by a rain of torpedo bombs from the air.

less. Only history will be his judge. To us he was a delightful dinner companion, a charming host, and a spectacular public performer.

In 1921, after his term of office as governor, Tasker Oddie was also elected to the United States Senate, and served two terms. Although Tasker and Key were frankly opposed to one another on almost every issue — especially the silver legislation — in controversies where the welfare of Nevada was involved, they worked together as one man. This was notably true of the Hoover Dam negotiations. Tasker was also devoted to road-building. Thousands of miles of highways throughout the United States are enduring monuments to Senator Oddie's efforts.

After George Wingfield's tremendous success in Goldfield, he established a chain of banks across the state, through which he poured, in loans to livestock men and prospectors, the fabulous wealth he had acquired in mining. As the years went on, he engaged not only in mining but in cattle-raising and hotel operation. He was also a powerful behind-the-scenes figure in state politics. George Nixon, Wingfield's old partner, died while he was United States senator, and Tasker Oddie, then governor of Nevada, offered the appointment to Mr. Wingfield. But he preferred to remain a private citizen.

The state hummed with stories of George Wingfield's benefactions. Cattlemen without number would tell of personal loans he made that were never collected, and prospectors recalled innumerable grubstakes that came from his lavish hand.

After weathering the early years of the Great Depression, George Wingfield's banking empire collapsed. The failure was tremendous and complete. In subsequent years Mr. Wingfield struggled against a tide of ill luck, but at last his benefactions paid off. One day an old friend came into possession of a low-grade surface indication on Kelly Creek, near Winnemucca. His first act was to ride into Reno, where he took George Wingfield into partnership without a dime of investment. Thanks to the loyalty of his old friend, Mr. Wingfield rode the crest of another wave of prosperity.

Hugh's legal affiliations spread all over the state. We traveled when we attended meetings of the American Bar Association. We went on to New York for the theatrical season. With the advent of the Great War in Europe, Hugh became devoted to the cause of world peace, journeying first to Philadelphia to attend a conference that led to the formation of the League to Enforce Peace, then, as a member of the executive committee for the Pacific Coast, making endless speeches on behalf of the League in Nevada and California. Strong Republican though he was, Hugh supported President Woodrow Wilson in his fight for the League of Nations.

The crest of Hugh's wave at the American Bar began to roll in about this time. The president-elect of the American Bar Association for 1918, an Illinois judge, asked Hugh to speak at the next year's banquet.

Eastern lawyers, the judge said, thought that there were no lawyers with brains west of the Mississippi. He wanted to show them they were wrong by *selecting* a speaker from the extreme West. But after the invitation was voiced, we both sensed an unmistakable note of uncertainty in his attitude.

But when the occasion arrived, Hugh delivered his tribute to the western pioneer, "The Spirit of the West." I was immensely proud as little notes began coming to me from hand to hand while Hugh was still speaking: "This is great!" "Hugh's going fine!" "Hugh is stealing the show." And as I sat in front of the president of the association, the benevolent smile he bestowed on me told me he was not disappointed.

On our way home from the meetings that year, we stopped off in Washington. The evening we arrived, Mrs. Herbert Hoover asked us to dine with them. Mr. Hoover, a classmate of Hugh's at Stanford, had been appointed Food Administrator for the United States; one of the men he had selected to join his staff was J. C. Campbell, Hugh's former partner, and several of the other guests that night were known to Hugh from his Stanford days.

As WORLD WAR I kept rumbling nearer and nearer, rising fears gave way to firm convictions. When in April, 1917, the United States entered the war, Tonopah's men and women, like people in every other town and city, revealed unimagined capabilities. As our Tonopah boys left to enlist, marching to the railroad station behind the Miners' Union Band, the men on the sidelines cheered and the women bit back the tears.

While Hugh became a Four Minute Man and spoke at Liberty Loan drives, which followed each other in rapid succession all over the state, I was inducted into the Junior Red Cross. The division chairman for the Pacific Coast appointed me director in Tonopah, a position of which I was very proud. I taught every grade in the school to knit; the younger children made wash cloths, and the older classes made sweaters. The prize for the best sweater was won by an eleven-year-old boy.

Our young people also did their bit for the Belgian children. We held an organized drive for funds on Christmas Eve —"Glorified Roundup," I called it. Four groups of singers were carried in trucks to the compass corners of the community, whence they walked to a spot in the center of town singing "Silent Night," "Hail to the King," "Little Town of Bethlehem," and other old favorites. That Christmas Eve was bitterly cold, the wind was full of sleet, and the ground covered with snow. As the sweet young voices of the children floated out over the frosty air, hardly a house failed to respond to our knock. Many people, at their windows watching for us, opened doors and quickly thrust into the collectors' hands five-, ten-, and twenty-dollar gold pieces.

The most spectacular feat our town accomplished was to send an ambulance to France. The whole town was mobilized into the Tonopah Ambulance Regiment — the T.A.R. — and held a carnival at which we raised the necessary $3,000 in one night.

The war was a turning point in many areas of our lives. It was responsible for one step forward in American democracy that was illustrated graphically in Nevada. Social lines in Tonopah were never strictly drawn. It was one of the charms of the life. But in Reno, the old staid community, class distinctions were drawn along rigid lines, and the social upheaval there took on something of a comedy of manners.

Reno had two strictly-drawn and opposing groups: those who approved of the divorce laws enacted by the legislature and those who would have none of them. If you belonged to one group, or were even known to countenance its views, you were subject to criticism from the other. Feeling ran deep and strong. I heard more than one Reno woman say, in effect, "I don't care who she is; if she comes to Reno for a divorce, I will not meet her." The lines were only a little less rigid among the men.

Obviously, every woman was entitled to work in the Red Cross, and everybody did. Some were savagely snubbed, though many of these women were of unexceptionable social position. Gradually, devotion to the cause, excellent work pursued silently under difficult conditions, good manners, and generosity eroded the prejudice. The process was slow, but when the war ended, the barriers were no longer discernible.

There is an episode from the war years that was an exciting experience for me. When tanks were first perfected, people were very curious about them, so the government sent a few tanks touring the country as stimulus for the Liberty Loan Drives. They lumbered from city to city, hopping long distances on flatcars.

On the morning a tank was due in Tonopah, I received a telephone call from one of the loan drive committeemen telling me the tank had been inadvertently sidetracked at a distant junction and couldn't be hauled in until the next morning. But the three young officers who manned the tank were in town. Would I entertain them for the day?

After lunch we went over to Goldfield, visited some of the famous leases, the handsome homes that had been built there, and a notorious saloon, as well as the little plot of grass that cost the owner forty dollars a month to keep green. In the late afternoon we started back to Tonopah.

Desert roads were never very well defined. A road would be used until the rains cut into it; then a new road would be carved out alongside the old one by autos turning out to avoid mud holes or high centers. The two roads ran side by side for long distances, so that a driver couldn't always tell whether a car was in his groove or another until it was practically on top of him. A turn in the road would show him whether he or the other fellow would have to turn out.

This afternoon I was coming along at my usual desert clip — sixty or seventy miles an hour, since there was nothing to fall off, hit or run into. Suddenly an oncoming car loomed up in our path. I could no more have jumped the rut at the rate I was going than I could have lifted the car out of it by hand. Luckily, the auto approaching happened to be in a spot where the driver *could* turn out. Calmly he shifted into the next lane, and I flashed by like a comet.

Not a person in my car had moved. For a long time no one spoke. At last the khaki-clad, square-jawed lieutenant sitting at my right, his arm resting negligently along the back of the seat, drawled, "Well . . . I spent eight months in the Argonne in a tank. Before the war I was a racing driver. But I never got a bigger thrill than that!"

The next day the tank came into town and rolled up the main street. People stood in doors and windows gaping in awe at the ungainly monster. Up Brougher Avenue it crawled, trailing a crowd of men and boys, and stopped in front of our home. Switching its tail around, it disgorged the young lieutenant, who came to attention and saluted.

"Mrs. Brown," he said, "yesterday you took me for a ride in your car. Today I want to take you for a ride in mine." I accepted with alacrity.

The young man climbed in and crawled down into the extreme front, where the controls were; and then, as he directed, I swung into the turret, strapped myself into the swinging seat above him, closed the top, and set the screws.

Near our home was a crater, what remained of an old filled-in assessment hole. Down into this he plunged the tank, with me suspended above him. Switching the monster around the crater like a giant top, he brought it up the sides of the crater snorting in midair. By this time I was flat on my back. With a final grinding crash the tank flopped down and I resumed a vertical position. In thorough enjoyment of my unorthodox antics, the lieutenant occasionally turned to grin up at me.

He proceeded to take me over the roughest terrain he could find, over the dumps we had looked at the day before, down the gullies, up the mountain. I was too proud to admit it, but I got some painful bruises. When I crawled out, he saw my skinned elbows and was gallantly apologetic, but I wouldn't have missed that experience for anything.

By 1920 GOLDFIELD, as well as many of the less spectacular strikes like Manhattan, Rhyolite, Bullfrog, and Rawhide, was pretty much at the end of production. However, Tonopah was still jogging along as one of the biggest silver producers in the world.

Many old friends had left: Jen Stock had lost her husband and followed a sister to Los Angeles where, alas, she died in a traffic accident; Herman Albert accepted a position with the Federal Reserve Bank in San Francisco. Several of the lawyers and many of our most successful businessmen remained in Nevada but moved to Reno.

Our neighbors, Mrs. Hank Knight and her courtly husband, flashed across our vision in later years. One day I was walking on the lot at the Lasky Studio in Hollywood with my uncle Theodore Roberts, who was then a member of the movie colony, and suddenly I saw a familiar face under the poke bonnet of a typical pioneer woman. It was Mrs. Hank Knight! She told me she and Hank had become regular extras in western films, and I must say they were perfectly type-cast for such parts.

But the "old timers," the mine superintendents and the engineers, were still with us. They serve to prove the point that the pioneers of Tonopah were a different type of frontiersman. However, those who panned dirt for a day's wages along the streams of California frequently experienced the adventures so dear to the heart of the true westerner. One such happened to an unsuspecting gentleman who was equal to the situation — Fred L. Berry, who had come to Tonopah from San Francisco, where he had been Assistant District Attorney.

Fred was elected District Attorney of Nye County and was therefore in the center of our labor disputes. One day a man burst into his office, brandishing a sharp-pointed pick with a head of great striking weight, and shouted, "They're after me!"

Fred looked at him with a coolness he had learned to assume in other face-to-face encounters and asked laconically, "Who?"

"The company spies," the man yelled. "They've got a rope! They're going to hang me!"

"Aw, come now . . ." Fred began, but the man stepped toward him, pick upraised.

"And you're in with 'em," he roared. "I'll kill ya'."

Fred gazed at the man with his customary jovial smile, but made no move and said quietly, "Okay. First, let's go down and have a drink."

The blazing eyes softened to sheepish embarrassment. Slowly the man lowered the pick and muttered, "Okay."

The lawyer rose, put his arm over the man's shoulder, and they clattered down the stairs to the saloon. Over a few drinks they swapped yarns until Fred was able to signal the bartender. Presently the sheriff drifted into the saloon and enticed the man into his custody.

When I heard Fred tell this story, another lawyer was present. "Fred," he said, "I think it was kinda sneakin' of ya to talk that man out of killin' ya."

Distinctions continued to flow toward my husband. Governors of both Nevada and California repeatedly appointed him to the Commission on Uniform State Laws. In 1920 he was asked by Herbert Hoover to second the nomination of Mr. Hoover at the Republican National Convention, but much to our chagrin, the dark horse, Warren G. Harding, was nominated instead.

From the beginning of Hugh's active association with the American Bar, he had talked "session in San Francisco." Finally, through his efforts, the executive committee accepted the invitation of the California Bar for the 1922 convention.

Hugh decided this was our opportunity to repay the great debt of hospitality we owed to our eastern friends. A special train would be made up in Chicago to bring conferees to San Francisco, so it would be a simple matter to arrange a day's stopover at Truckee for a side trip to Lake Tahoe. In order to distinguish our guests — almost a hundred people — each person was given a sprig of sagebrush (which I had brought from Tonopah) as he stepped off the train. With this insignia, everything was at his disposal — golf, swimming, drinks, smokes. For lunch we served mountain trout or prairie chicken, and in the afternoon a big chartered launch took our guests for a tour of the lake. As the sun was going down, reflected in the opalescent water, everyone returned to the train, and San Francisco.

In 1920 Hugh's name had been one of four placed in nomination for the presidency of the American Bar, the first time any western lawyer had been so considered. Also when a vacancy occurred on the Supreme Court of the United States, Hugh's friends in Nevada joined a host of fellow members of the American Bar Association in presenting his name to President Harding as a candidate. The letters of endorsement from almost every state, together with the glowing responses from the Nevada newspapers, were a heartening experience for both of us.

But, for a number of years, we had been aware that Hugh's health, never robust, was being undermined by some internal threat. His strength could not have borne the burdens of these responsibilities, and so when the proposed honors were unproductive, we were content.

Tonopah geologists made models of their mines. On thin glass slides, some of which hung vertically in slender grooves while others lay horizontally on tiny cleats, all the workings of the mine were traced to scale in colored inks. When you stood in front of the model and looked into its serried sections, you seemed to be looking into the earth with a magic eye. Here the shaft dropped down from level to level through ore and country rock; here were "drifts" and "stopes" and "crosscuts" with every foot of ore blocked out; and here you traced the meandering vein, noted where it petered out or widened into richness unimagined as it continued into regions still unexplored.

They were beautiful things, these glass models, made by skilled craftsmen, often works of art. When I think of Tonopah, the memory is like such a model of a life I was privileged to live, unique and gone: the humble water carrier who brought his precious cargo to my door in a barrel; the old Indian who had been a warrior and carried himself with such dignity; the prospector who picked up a rock to throw at a burro and discovered ore that poured millions into hands he never saw; the men who were made by its magic or were ruined by its power; the cowboy who read philosophy and the gambler who was godfather to a state; the men and women who touched my hand and warmed my heart; and last of all, the view from the top of the world when I rode on a roundup. These things, so full of meaning for me, were a vein of ore whose richness increased with depth.

So we were approaching the end of the spectacular years in Tonopah. The single year that Hugh had planned to stay had stretched into twenty. Our sons had completed high school and were about to enter Stanford University in Palo Alto, California. We decided to leave the desert and make our home in Palo Alto.

The trunks were locked and ready for the expressman. All of our possessions were crated and gone. I had just one more errand, to ship a box of particular treasures by Wells Fargo. This errand accomplished,

I turned away from the counter when the manager stepped out of his tiny office and came toward me.

"You're Mrs. Hugh Brown, aren't you?"

"Yes," I replied. Strange coincidence, I had heard the same words just before I arrived in Tonopah as a bride, spoken with the same falling inflection that answered itself. Now, almost at the moment of leaving, they were being said to me again.

"They tell me you're an old-timer around here." The man smiled as he looked me over. "You certainly don't look like a pioneer."

"Oh, but I am," I answered proudly. "I came here on a stagecoach in February, 1904."

"Somebody told me I ought to look you up. I wish I had been here in the beginning," he added with a note of regret. "This place is all that is left of the old West, isn't it?"

"It's a fusion of the old West and the new. Tonopah has become awfully metropolitan with our brick buildings and concrete pavements. Now even the prospectors use Fords." But, we agreed, the new West attracted the same kind of friendly, unpretentious people as the old.

Now the actual moment of departure was at hand. Outside, the boys were strapping bags to the trunk rack of the old Hudson touring car, with little sister bossing the job. Hugh and I stood alone in the empty 'Dobe Shack, which had held so much of fulfillment. As my hand sought his, I thought of that nineteen-year-old girl who stepped off the stage coach into Boomtown twenty years ago. I thought of my uncle's beckoning words toward fame and how they haunted me in those tragic middle years, and I offered a little prayer of gratitude to the unknown person who said, "Home-keeping hearts are happiest." Then we shut the door, joined the noisy children, and sped away down the hill.